Growing Up Christian
in the
Twenty-First Century

Douglas W. Johnson

Judson Press® Valley Forge

GROWING UP CHRISTIAN IN THE TWENTY-FIRST CENTURY

Copyright © Douglas W. Johnson, 1984
Published by Judson Press, Valley Forge, PA 19482-0851

Library of Congress Cataloging in Publication Data

Johnson, Douglas W., 1934–
  Growing up Christian in the twenty-first century.

  Bibliography: p.
  1. Christian life—1960–   2. Twenty-first
century—Forecasts.   I. Title.
BV4509.5.J64 1984   248.4   84-15452
ISBN 0-8170-1048-3

The name JUDSON PRESS is registered as a trademark in the U.S. Patent Office.
Printed in the U.S.A. ⊕

Dedicated to
Phyl, a working wife and mother,
and to our daughters
Heather, Kirsten, and Tara

Preface

Looking into the future is scary because what we see is beyond our ability to control, and most of us like to live in settings over which we can exercise approval or veto power. Aging and death, two facts of the future, come without either our approval or veto. Young people who are in our care today will be caring for us in one way or another in two or three decades. As time progresses, roles change, and dependencies and authorities shift. Sobering reality suggests that the future is one change after another.

The girl with whom we journey twenty-five years in this book is in our homes today. We will name her Jill. We see her as a child, a reflection of our values and ambitions. As we take the trip described in this book, we will discover roles for ourselves that we never contemplated. The journey will underscore our immediate tasks as well as those we will undertake in the next decade. We of the church have a lot to do if this young person is to have the foundation of values that she will need by the time she reaches her early thirties. The trip lays out an agenda of growth not only for her but for us and our churches.

The disciplines of projecting and thinking about events two-and-a-half decades in the future have been helpful to me. I make no claim that every child, male or female, will have the experiences outlined in this book. My aims have been to expose decision points in a life and to indicate how parents, peers, and churches interact and influence those choices. I hope you will find the journey as fascinating and hopeful as I have.

Douglas W. Johnson
Ridgewood, New Jersey
March 1984

Contents

ONE

Introduction

Change is a necessary part of life. Nothing within us or in the world surrounding us is kept for tomorrow exactly as it is today. Our minds and bodies begin life weak, grow strong, and become weak once again as we travel life's span. Human frailty, however, is not focused on individuals. Societies and social groups change as well. In fact, much of what we feel as pressure on our individual lives is due to shifts in the expectations and behavior patterns of our society.

Studying and trying to understand social change has been a challenge for me for several years. I began this study in graduate school, and then in late 1968 I combined it with the discipline of futuring. In the fall of 1968, a few months after completing a dissertation in which I sought to develop a model for predicting social change, I was introduced to futuring through an address by a staff member of the Hudson Institute. As a result of that experience, I was introduced to the surprise free future, the theme of Herman Kahn and the Institute. In the years following, the theory underlying their theme became part of my intellectual perceptions.

Kahn's work emphasized continuity in human experience rather than focusing on cataclysmic events as primary determinants of society's future direction. My resonance with this theory is the reason I found Alvin Toffler's *Future Shock* less helpful than his *The Third Wave*. Both Toffler books address our future, but the second is more in keeping with a view of continuity and cyclical nature of human experience than is the first.

Social change and futuring became more focused for me in 1973 when, in early December, I heard Arnold Mitchell of Stanford Research International (then known as Stanford Research Institute) tell of research he and colleagues were conducting on societal value structures.[1] The group was creating a societal model using a sophisticated recasting of Abraham Maslow's hierarchy of needs. For me the most powerful concept of their research was the life pattern. Their work states that people base their lives on certain values and, as a result, create an identifiable life pattern. The word "life-style" is more limiting than "life pattern" because it denotes the way in which people relate to the world around them, not the value base guiding those relationships. A life pattern is the foundation stone upon which a life is based, and the term is used frequently in this book to describe Jill's basis for acting.

The Third Wave, by Alvin Toffler, and *America Tomorrow*, edited from reports in *The Wall Street Journal* (1977) by Donald Moffitt, have contributed a sense of realism to the future projections. I am indebted to their approach for the kinds of future events Jill faces in this book.

Basic assumptions in the following presentation include the belief that humans are tough and resilient and that people adapt quickly to changing economic situations, energy shortfalls, and natural disasters. They may revise their timetables for accomplishing tasks but tend to continue to follow their values.

This book doesn't deal with economic rises and falls per se. It assumes that in every person's life there are good times and bad. The values of life, however, are not swayed as easily as are life-styles. Life-styles are dependent on economics. The life-changing decisions that Jill makes are realistic given the choices of values and the life pattern by which she lives. Her timetable for decision making shifts somewhat, but this is normal for most people.

Jill, the girl we follow through this book, is limited in her

[1] This research was presented in a paper entitled "Life Ways, Futures, and Markets" in the J.C. Penney Forum.

range of choices by decisions made today by people she will never know or meet. For instance, many builders in the late 1970s decided that the combined costs of materials, labor, and energy were too high to sustain large tracts of single family houses. They decided to concentrate their resources on building apartments, row houses, and condominiums. This was a reversal of thinking that turned thousands of square miles of land around cities into look-alike suburban developments. This limits Jill's options for housing when she is ready to find a place to live.

The women's movement is another force from the 1970s that will continue to affect Jill's life. Significant changes in attitudes about women's roles and capabilities have taken place already and will open new possibilities for young women like Jill when they go to college and begin careers. Equal pay, child-care centers, prekindergarten schooling, part-time jobs, and work-at-home opportunities are trends that will be enforced and expanded by experience in the decades ahead. The women's movement has been and will be the most powerful force reshaping society in the United States and around the world during Jill's lifetime.

This book also assumes that Jill can implement her decision to attend college and prepare for a career. College costs are frighteningly high now, and there is little hope for a downturn in the near future. Yet people seem to be able to put together the resources to secure such training. Community college and state college networks have been a boon to many by providing alternatives to higher priced private schools. College was for a small elite until the GI bill opened college to veterans after World War II. Since then the assumption has been made that anyone who wants to attend college can. While this has never been true, Jill's desires and her parents' knowledge of how to secure needed financial resources will help her to prepare for her chosen career.

Those who have followed the impact of the personal computer on people and business will recognize its importance in Jill's life. As a technology, the personal computer will do for Jill's generation what the automobile did for previous generations. Freedom from much of the drudgery of life and work are only two of the benefits of this little machine. Rapid exchange of information, the ability to work while living far from one's work place, and access to data that previously had been available only in specialized libraries are three factors Jill will capitalize on as she pursues her career. The constraints of commuting and being close to a data source will not be hers. She will enjoy a freedom from place that her parents did not.

We will meet Jill's parents at various times in the book. They will be part of the population bulge of older persons at the end of the century. (See *U. S. News & World Report*, [Nov. 22, 1982].) They will enjoy pensions not tied to a company. Their pensions will be funded partly by companies and partly by themselves in plans administered by financial institutions. The introduction of IRAs, reforms in the Social Security system, and the need for companies to be relieved of some nonessential costs, will result in the management of pensions by currently nontraditional forms. Even if this doesn't happen in quite the way I visualize, Jill's parents will have opportunities to work part time, mobility, and adequate income at the normal age of retirement.

Career change will be a product of personal interest and necessity. Technological advancement will make some occupations obsolete, and foreign competition in the marketplace will eliminate jobs in some industries. Working for the same company for a lifetime is not now, nor will it be for Jill, a value. The primary value on which Jill's career is based is personal self-fulfillment. She will be doing something in which she is interested and in which she can make a contribution. This means that an individual's career takes precedence over loyalty to an institution or a business. Jill, in this book, uses her working parents as her model when she contemplates career change.

International politics will impinge on Jill as they influence everyone daily. The oil embargo forced a review of energy consumption habits and produced a conserving life pattern for our society. Jill picked this pattern up from her parents and will live by it even though another oil embargo may never occur. Prices of coffee, tea, and chocolate rose sharply in the late 1970s and early 1980s, and many people stopped using them. Health-conscious individuals began to find alternatives to these bev-

erages, and by the time Jill becomes an adult, their use will be
even more limited.

Terrorism is and will be an abomination, but many people
all over the world live with it daily. They do not drastically
adjust their lives except to be more cautious with strangers and
more security minded at home. Life, for most people, is to be
lived, even though it may end at any moment. It is unlikely
that Jill will do much more than take some instruction in self-
defense while she is in college and install a security device or
system in her apartment or home. She may adjust travel plans
when there seems to be a danger of terrorist activities. In general, she will not be part of a police state or social mentality
in which everyone is continually frightened by the possibility
of a terrorist attack.

War and the threat of war is a human condition. Many would
like to change this, but the likelihood of making much headway
in this area seems remote during the time we will be with Jill.
A few experts in the Delphi project (see Resources at end of
book) believe that a major war might erupt before the end of
this century. However, most experts don't foresee a major war
but believe that limited wars will continue to occur in many
different nations. The effect of these conflagrations on Jill will
be direct only when someone she knows is sent to or volunteers
to serve in the armed forces in one of these war zones.

The production of weaponry is a cyclical activity of govern-
ments. Their defense budgets rise and fall rather than continue
a constant percentage of their gross national products. Given
the need to restructure the world's economy, a general reduction
in such costs worldwide might occur during Jill's early adulthood.

The cost of government entitlements, such as Social Security,
federal employee pensions, medicare, veterans benefits, college
expense loans, food stamps, and hundreds of other items, will
be reduced during Jill's growing-up years. The financial security
system that has been paid for through taxes will increasingly
be made a cooperative system, with the individual picking up
more costs. Jill will feel the consequences of these decisions as
she thinks about health care and pensions at the beginning of
her career.

As we read about Jill's life during the next quarter century, these articulated assumptions will be evident. You may want to pursue some of the resources listed at the conclusion of this book to determine the bases for these assumptions.

It's going to be an interesting life that we follow. As we follow Jill, let's look carefully at the impact of the church on this young person. The church is where we can do things that make a difference to her over the long run.

TWO

Pressures
in Today's World

The pressures of today's world do not directly affect an eight-year-old girl. The following adult comments illustrate pressures that adults suppose an eight year old faces.

"Jill's sitting on the couch watching TV. She's mixed up. She wants to belong to Girl Scouts but is too young. She doesn't like Brownies because the kids are too small. Would you talk to her, please? Maybe you can help her make a decision."

"As a parent, you know your child better than I, but let me give you some general observations about third graders. Third grade is a transitional time for eight and nine year olds. This year they move from being very young children to children with ideas and thoughts of their own that they can verbalize. We teachers help them through this phase in many ways, two of which you will hear about very soon. We cut out recess, and we give them more homework."

"More than a third of the children in this community in grades one through three live in a situation that is a product of a divorce. In most instances the children seem to have adjusted well, but in several cases, dormant discipline problems have surfaced since the divorce. The children need the help that a stable family setting could provide, but there just isn't stability in the family."

"Fantasies, ghosts, and spirits are realities to the eight and nine year old. When TV runs horror shows, these children should not be allowed to watch. They are too impressionable. They may not talk about their feelings, but the fright or fear of death and the unknown are exaggerated for them. You have to set viewing rules."

"We want our young elementary students, up to third grade, to become computer literate. We want them to know how to use the computer, and, for those most interested, we offer instruction in beginning computer programming. They have a lifetime ahead of them, and they will have to know and use computers. We want to do our part to make them ready to use such technology."

There are other pressures on a child although the child understands them not as the social change they are but in terms of how they affect the child. For instance, a child of eight comprehends population shifts from the northeastern and north central states to the southern and southwestern states in terms of classmates who move away. She doesn't know how important these population changes have been for adults whose jobs and housing are affected. She isn't aware because she doesn't have to make decisions about jobs and housing.

A significant trend in the mid-1980s has been the increase in the number of unrelated couples who live together. Our eight year old is acquainted with this phenomenon through her friends' brothers and sisters who have apartments and live-in arrangements.

She learns about the trend of later marriage by observing and listening to adults talk. It seems natural to her that her friends' older brothers and sisters who are working are not married yet. She doesn't realize that her parents were married at a much younger age than most of them.

Computers, cable television, video-cassette recorders, satellite communication, and telephoning to various places in the world are part of her everyday world. After all, these have existed and have been used for as long as she can remember. She doesn't understand the social adjustments that adults have had to make because of these technologies. She has been aware of such things for fewer than five years. Most of these technological changes have had a commercial life span of not much longer than that.

Three of her friends have trouble speaking English. They speak other languages. She is excited when they tell about their distant homelands and how they ate and lived differently than she. Her friends are refugees whose homes in other nations have become a memory. They are among the millions who have changed Jill's society because they sought this land in which to live.

Jill likes to travel and isn't conscious of its costs. She knows that flying is too expensive for her family and that her family travels mostly by auto. She sees several of her classmates going to other parts of the world and thinks it would be great if her family could travel like them. But she is satisfied to go away twice a year on auto trips. She thinks everyone goes away from home on trips.

Later she may understand the difference between affluence and poverty. At this age, she would not completely comprehend the contrast between them. Yet her trips to the nearby city have revealed mixes of cultures, races, and housing. These mixes are elements of another world for her. She is protected from facing such mixes as reality in her limited social world.

Jill, as an eight year old, does not think about social change because she has no basis for comparing the present with the past. Her concerns are with family, school, and neighborhood. Social change to her means handling changing friendships.

Yet she, with an emerging individuality and some changing perceptions of reality, is the hope of tomorrow. In twenty-five years she and/or some of her classmates will be leaders in education, government, business, and church. They will be nearly thirty when the century changes and will have upon their shoulders increasing responsibilities for raising their own children, teaching new generations, and reasserting their values in times of crises.

An adult examining a class picture of a school's third grade class will need to look beyond the missing teeth, pigtails, and scrubbed faces if he or she wants to see and understand the social forces that will shape their future. At the end of the twenty-five-year time frame of this book, the children may resemble their earlier pictures in a physical sense, but they will have acquired a basis for making social decisions in a changing world. This foundation will be theirs because of the efforts of teachers, parents, and peers.

Church leaders, therefore, need to realize that they are not "working with children" so much as they are helping to shape a future as they program for and train eight and nine year olds. These children will grow and mature. Life doesn't allow children to remain young. They grow and, in the Christian scenario, assume their responsible role in God's creation.

The beauty of this scenario is that the church has an opportunity to influence and guide children as they mature. Because the church is a human institution, it often doesn't do a very good job influencing and guiding children. It is by the grace of God and hours of work by dedicated church school teachers, youth leaders, choir leaders, pastors, and parents that children who go to church grow up to be Christians.

Helping these young people grow up to be Christians is a group effort. The phrase "the Christian community" signifies that each church member has responsibility for the moral, spiritual, and ethical education of children and young people. Teaching and being a positive role model are not tasks only of parents or of church school teachers.

Instilling the values that Jill will need to withstand the trials of the coming years is a difficult task. It will be necessary to explain, explain, and explain again the meaning and purpose of life as the realities of illness, death, accident, success, fame, and misfortune impinge upon the developing individual. She will need a great deal of love and comfort to cure the loneliness and ease the feelings resulting from tragedies that are common fare in life. Her parents must be surrounded with support and concern as they grapple with daily problems posed by Jill's inquiring activities.

A child may be a gift of God but every gift exacts a price. One part of the price of having a child is that adults are required to give responsible care to help her successfully confront changes in the society of which she is a part. Much will be demanded of those in whose shadows the child walks. The adults with whom the child lives, plays, and works need humility and patience, two of God's gifts. Those who want to influence the child toward God must have personal direction, purpose, and solid Christian values. Those who want the child to hear them must be willing to listen and learn.

As we follow Jill for a twenty-five year flight ahead in time, we will recognize her need for the church during every one of those years as she makes decisions that solidify her life pattern in the midst of social flux. One of those individual choices will be whether she will or will not create a family.

As adults, our journey will be a sobering one because during that same quarter century our roles will reverse. She will become the teacher and we the students. She will be the future hope, and we will be her link to a past and, it is hoped, to a stable foundation of values. We will take on the role of supporter as she assumes the leadership functions we pass on to her.

Her life, and ours, is governed by an interaction of internal and external forces. While her personal development is important, most of our attention will be on the social forces Jill will encounter at specific decision points in life. Social change as it affects a girl growing up to be a Christian is our theme.

At the beginning of Jill's life, we make decisions on her behalf before she is aware of the social implications of choices. As she grows, she will be able to choose alternatives in her social situation. We and she are social beings. What it means to be a social being with a Christian purpose is our next concern.

A Social Entity

No one is an individual apart from a supporting cast of people. George H. Mead[1] said that an individual's social personality develops as one continually adjusts to the perceptions of others. This is one way of stating that every person is a social entity. We are affected by cues from both internal and external parts of our being as we create and react to social situations. People learn early in life how to handle social change, and it continues to be an essential element of life for everyone.

A child of eight has been exposed to many social stimuli. She has attended formal school at least two and perhaps for as many as five years. She has been part of a community and/or church organization that has taught cooperation and values.

[1] George H. Mead, *Mind, Self and Society.* Charles Morris, ed. (Chicago: University of Chicago Press, 1934).

She has lived with parents or adults who have attempted to care for her physical, social, and psychological needs. She has been allowed to play at make believe, she has learned to work at simple tasks; and she has been taught how to dress for and behave in various kinds of situations.

A child is a social entity. That means that several persons and groups are influential in forming her values and life pattern. She needs adult assistance in these tasks, and those adults who are most loving and caring toward her will have lasting import on her life. At the vulnerable age of eight, she can be swayed from one set of values to another by adults who can manipulate immature feelings.

The church, viewing a child as a social entity, knows that its programs can influence that child. The persons who lead and teach children will have more influence on future life patterns than they can begin to appreciate. In spite of the evident fidgeting and socializing with others that eight year olds do during class and choir rehearsals, they are learning the values and attitudes of their leaders and teachers. Leaders and teachers are dealing with young people who are absorbing the attitudes and the expressions of leaders as much as they are absorbing the content of the materials being presented. Therefore, the way that adult Christians cope with social change provides a model to children. Children see how to act as Christians.

When one recognizes the impact of a social model on a child, that indicates that one has an awareness of the influence of the social environment on her maturation. The society can interact with the child and her internal values and feelings through the years to produce an adult Christian. The church must be part of her environment in order to instill and challenge the child's intellect and values. The church must help her to handle feelings, especially as she is involved in life-changing experiences. A child is an adult at the beginning of life. The church by influencing the child will help to shape the values and life pattern of the adult.

Society's Stake in the Child

A society has a physical, social, and economic stake in each child. Society depends on its children to continue its history.

The importance of this dependence is illustrated in the ways a society encourages their birth, supervises their education, protects their interests, and puts before them options for their future.

Physical

Society depends upon, and many societies encourage, couples to produce children. Each society must continually replace its dying generations. It does this by encouraging the creation and ensuring the growth and training of new generations. In other words children must be born, educated, trained, and merged into the flow of everyday life. However, procreation is the most critical element in this sequence. Careful monitoring by a society of its marriages, births, and deaths is not just a statistical procedure. It is a necessary means of keeping tabs on a society's future viability. A child is not only an individual but is a vital extension into the future for a society.

The decision to have children is a private one; however, societal influences affect individual decisions. When having children is regarded by society as a good sign or as a necessary means of continuing a family name, individuals who have decided not to have children may change their minds. When business begins to find ways to care for children while parents are at work, this becomes societal affirmation for having children. When public media promote ideals relating to parenthood, society is telling people that having children is good. Social pressure to have children comes from peer groups as well as family and public media. In effect, any society is maintained by people living out group values, and when one of the strongest of these is to make certain there will be people in the future, parenthood will be affirmed.

Social

The importance of children to a society can be measured by the degree of concern society places on children's development. In our society, for example, much public money and public support ensure protection of children and their healthy growth. Educational institutions have been established, are supported, and are upgraded to give young people a grounding in the skills and ethics of the society. Religious institutions are encouraged to provide opportunities for children to learn traditions and beliefs that will contribute to the stability of the society. Courts are available to make certain that children, if abused or neglected, can be taken from parents and given to others who will provide a more healthy environment. Children are encouraged to take part in recreational activities so that they will become strong and be able to withstand the rigors of competition, which are a normal part of society. Society supports hospitals that specialize in treating and curing childhood afflictions. Doctors train to work with children so that the mortality rate continues to diminish. Societal institutions protect the physical, social, and value aspects of young people from birth onward. A society that wants its children to mature pays attention not only to physical but also to other parts of the developing lives of children.

Society protects and trains its offspring. This doesn't mean that society is benevolent and indulgent to children. It demands from them respect for its traditions, willingness to protect societal institutions, adherence to a basic set of values, and acceptance of their need to produce additional children. Children may be regarded as gifts in the order of life, but they are needed. In addition, children bring with them burdens and responsibilities for parents and other members of society.

Economic

Society's economic stake in children is high. The economic investment is as crucial as the need to train young people to uphold societal values and traditions. Children create both markets and jobs. They need clothes, food, recreational and educational facilities and materials, playthings, entertainment activities, instruments, and a host of other related materials and activities. The needs or supposed needs of young people create markets that are crucial to a society's continued economic viability.

For example, the baby boom of the 1950s immediately increased the number of jobs in construction and education because more schools and teachers were needed. These same babies, as they have grown, have produced highly skilled workers for the affluent era of the 1980s. The matured babies have become workers and consumers and have triggered a basic change in the economics of this society. A child is not just a precious bundle to parents but an important economic addition for a society.

Society is not an uninterested bystander when a child is born. Society has a self-interest in the child. Thus, social institutions spend much time, money, and energy in making certain that the child is raised according to specific standards. While the prevailing social standards may allow the child freedom to become an individual, the core values of society are passed on through educational curricula, state accreditation of teachers, and state-approved standards of competence for other professionals. The state, created and governed by laws reflecting common values held by its citizens, does not rigidly impose its will but sets boundaries and establishes guidelines to assure a child's development in a pattern consistent with societal goals.

By the time the child has reached eight years of age, society's stake has increased considerably. Much money has been spent on education, recreation, entertainment, and value formation. Traditions have been discussed and have become a part of the child's belief system. The need for various kinds of institutions and professions has been demonstrated for, and accepted by, the child. Parents have been equipped with value-oriented training to ensure that the child is trained in ways acceptable to society. This investment of a society in the child will continue through a lifetime, but the early molding is nearly completed by the child's eighth birthday. Society's stake will increase some more, but in a few years society's torch will be carried by this person. Society works the hardest during the first eight years of a child's life to instill in the child the basic beliefs that it feels are essential for society's continuation.

The Child as Product

It may sound crass, but a child is a product. She is a physical product of parents, but, more important for society, she is a social product of parents, school, peers, other adults, and social institutions. While each individual brings uniqueness to life, that person's inherent capabilities and tendencies are encouraged or suppressed by those persons and institutions with which the child comes in contact. For instance, in the early years of the twentieth century a black youth who wanted to be a major-league baseball player was denied that opportunity by societal practices. This didn't deny the individual's capabilities and skills but made it impossible for the young person to achieve acclamation by playing in the major leagues. No black players were allowed in major baseball leagues until 1947. Society had to change before black youth could realistically expect to be major league ball players.

Being a product does not deny individual initiative. A person adjusts and grows because of social forces that challenge in one direction and deny in another. If one road is closed, a person may choose another. It is at the point of choosing and deciding between social alternatives that individual values and intellect are used the most. A suggestion from parents or peers may be the most influential factor in a particular choice, but the actual decision of which option to take is up to the person. It is important for church leaders to realize that at points of indi-vidual choice a person makes a decision on the basis of what others, including church-leaders, have contributed in experi-ence and insight to that individual.

The quality of one's social background, in this case the in-fluence of education, peers, parents, and other persons who make up a child's social environment, is important to the future direction open to any child. For example, a baby born in a poverty-stricken home in the valleys of Appalachia is often socially disadvantaged in comparison to a child born to a Co-lumbia University professor in New York City. The individual capabilities of the two children may be approximately the same, but the social influences and pressures on them will be quite different. The products of the two distinct social environments can be worlds apart within eight years of their births. Social components affecting children are of great importance. What's inside a child is important but is not most determinative. Rather what a child becomes results from a combination of internal gifts and external opportunities.

The possible loss of creativity to society, evident in this illustration, is one reason society tries to upgrade those situations with fewer advantages. Society recognizes deficiencies in the social support systems for some children. The larger community tries to make up such lacks so that potential leaders will be found and supported. A life is too important to waste, and society has acknowledged that fact in such ways as providing scholarship aid to colleges, promoting busing of school children to ensure equal educational opportunities during elementary and high school years, and providing adult retraining opportunities as well as education. Society wants its people to be useful.

The Church's Stake in the Child

The church's interest in a child, especially if she is part of a church member's household, is similar to society's interest. This interest includes physical, social, and economic aspects although these are measured somewhat differently by the church than by society.

The church, just like society, needs people to replace dying generations if it is to have a future. Physically the number of children from which to recruit members will indicate and maybe determine the long-term future of a congregation or a church. In this sense, a child is welcomed into the world for the same reason society welcomes her, as an insurer of the future. In a different sense, every child in society can be regarded as a potential member of a church. This potential can be realized when the church proclaims its beliefs through public media.

A church must believe its convictions about the way life is to be lived. It must expect that the eternal aspects of human existence that it preaches and teaches have universal appeal. A congregation must feel and act as though everyone in its community can benefit from its message and life pattern. If it doesn't believe this, the congregation hasn't anything distinctive to share.

The church's physical stake in children is selfish. Without children the church would have no future. An exception is the Shakers, a denomination that does not encourage the birth of children. The denomination has been able to survive by acquiring converts. This survival, however, has been precarious and is not an example for other religious groups. Children have and will continue to be a means of growth and maintenance of membership for most churches and congregations.

The economic aspect of the church's stake in young people is similar to that of society. Children create jobs in the church for educators, printers, church builders, equipment makers, and clergy. Educational, devotional, and informative materials produced by most religious publishers for children are important economically. This economic importance does not minimize the conviction that children must be trained in Christian values and life patterns, a conviction that most publishers and teachers hold. However, not to understand the economic implications of these convictions is to deny an important social truth, namely that societies and churches exist in an economic atmosphere.

The church can be most influential in designing training that meets the developmental needs of young people. This is the area in which the church has its greatest stake in a child. The training process begins at birth and costs much in time, money, and energy. Children must learn the message, memorize the catechisms, become acquainted with the symbols, understand the history, and develop a particular life pattern if they are to become useful members of a congregation and a church. In this regard, the church has long-term goals as reasons for devoting so much effort to families.

Congregations are the nests in which Christian fellowship and training occur. The church, because of its limited time with children, depends on parents to add to and enforce the training given to children while they are at the church building.

Because it wants to spread its message, the church assumes responsibility for finding adequate teachers and role models to accomplish the training it wants to provide for young people. Finding such models is never completely satisfying since the church must be content with people who aren't perfect. A part of the church's responsibility, therefore, is to have several people who can become a composite social role model. These persons include a pastor, church school teacher, choir members, and nonclergy worship leaders. The social model that emerges from these individuals can assist young people to determine how best to live according to the life pattern the church requires.

Church leaders and teachers must be versed in the history

and traditions of the Christian faith as well as in the particular church in which the child finds herself. Assisting leaders to develop personal prayer and devotional habits is another responsibility of the church. How can church members teach unless they can apply what they teach to their own lives?

The church's stake in a child is enormous, but its responsibility is equally large. The price of accepting a child into the fellowship of the church includes educating the child, providing fellowship opportunities, assisting the parents, and training leaders who will influence the child's development. These costs are borne willingly by most congregations because they ensure the existence of the church in the future.

The Child's Reactions

How often parents have tried and failed to get their children to attend church school regularly! When they refuse, parents wonder what has gone wrong. The problem is not easy to pinpoint since a child's decision to attend church school is based on his or her own feelings and subtle reactions about the church picked up from parents and peers. The parents may not personally like the child's teacher at church school. The child picks up this dislike from parental comments. Peers at school and peer models on television may suggest that going to church is a waste of time or of no value to a child. Also the child may find the materials and teaching methods used at church boring and not challenging.

A child reacts, at age eight, on the basis of parental and peer pressures. Most of her reactions are rooted in interaction from within the home. "Do as I do" is the model she responds to most positively. She isn't given to listening or acting on the basis of philosophical or theological reasoning. She mimics what she sees and if her parents aren't interested, neither will she be inclined to attend church or church school.

Consequently, the church's efforts in educating, training, and activating the child's parents are reflected in the child's interest or disinterest in the church. If the effort has been minimal, the child will be uninterested. If the church has interested the parents, the child will be positively inclined. When a child is eight years old, she and her parents come into the church together. When this family package is brought into the church, negative images from peers and mass media can be offset.

The child is a social creature, and the church is a social institution. The commitment of those in the church as well as their preparation to lead and teach others will have a great effect on the church's ability to influence the child as well as the parents. The church exerts one of several social pressures the child feels, and it must compete well if it is to enhance and help direct the future of the child. The opportunity to influence the child carries with it significant responsibilities regarding the selection and training of adult leaders as well as generating and sustaining programs that accomplish the church's purpose of spreading the gospel to new generations.

Congregations willing to offset disparaging images gotten from television can interest children and parents. Churches must struggle against social forces to get and keep the attention of members and potential members. To feel that the church's message is powerful enough without personal witnessing to it is foolishness. People change because those around them exert pressure on them to change. The church must use its own means of generating social pressures to keep people aware of its programs and activities. Church leaders and clergy must visit church members in order to keep them interested. This is especially true for reaching eight year olds who do as they are told more often than being able to do as they wish.

THREE

Early Teen
Pressures in 1990

The eight year old of the mid-1980s was shaped by a world characterized by an increasing number of divorces in her friends' families, an affluence that allowed her to acquire many things older generations would have considered unnecessary, an ethic promoting conservation of environment and resources as well as money and energy, and an emphasis on the need for personal stability.

It may have seemed contradictory to talk of family stability when so many divorces were granted in the mid-1980s. Yet the need for a stable environment in which young people could grow and develop was evident. In many situations, stability was sought in homes as the two divorced parents tried to retain normalcy for their children. Children of divorced parents remained Jill's friends even though, after their parents' final separation, some became obnoxious or whiny or louder and more boisterous than before. Jill tried to act the same toward them in spite of their difficult behavior. She recognized in her own way that these young friends needed her more now then they might have in the past.

As an eight year old, she had been aware that the brother of one of her friends shared an apartment with two other men even though he was in his midtwenties. She had wondered why his parents wanted him to get married. He seemed happy the way he was. The girl-friends he brought home were nice.

29

She didn't think he wanted to get married. As he said, "Why rush things, Mom? I like to be free of those kinds of obligations. Maybe later I'll get interested." Jill thought that maybe she would live with some girls when she got old enough.

She didn't understand the dramatic gains in life expectancy that had been made by the mid-1980s. Better health care, more attention to illnesses, and life-easing technologies were combining to lengthen people's lives. She would live to be nearly eighty if she had a normal life while her parents were projected to live into their early or midseventies. Neither did she appreciate that the infant mortality rate declined between 1960 and the mid-1980s. This wouldn't be a concern to her until much later, but it did affect her friends' mothers as they decided whether or not to have an additional child. Her perception of longevity was having two sets of grandparents whom she visited twice each year.

She traveled with the family often in the mid-1980s and especially looked forward to evenings in a motel. She accepted the traveling pattern even though she knew her parents were not rich. Everyone she knew seemed to go away for vacations twice a year. Many liked to camp, but her parents preferred staying in motels. It seemed natural to go places rather than to stay at home all the time.

The school she attended had a computer for each grade level. It was used as a teaching tool, and, by age eight, she had done some programming and learning with it. Several of her friends had computers at home, but her parents couldn't see the need for having one of their own.

If someone had told her that she was the child of an affluent age, she would have been confused. Having enough food to eat, a home in which to live, and a car to travel in didn't seem unusual to her. She was part of a social environment that considered these things normal aspects of living. She did help collect food and toys for children who didn't have as much as she, but none of her friends were the recipients. She knew young people at school whose clothes sometimes needed a patch and whose shoes were beyond scuffing. She didn't view them as underprivileged; they just had a different life pattern than she.

That was when she was eight. Now it is 1990, and she is in her early teens. She has learned more about life. She knows that the neighbors across the street are without a father. He comes home occasionally, but in talking with the neighbor's daughter who is a year older than she, Jill understands that a divorce is in the works. It is upsetting to her because her friend, the neighbor girl, is emotionally distraught on many days. Jill is more aware of the hurt and confusion of her friend now than she was when her other friends had been part of a divorce a few years ago.

She has learned about role models, and she has learned to stand up for herself. For instance, some boys tried to keep her from playing baseball on a neighborhood team, but she persisted. She turned out to be a better player than some of them.

She is looking forward to a career or at least a job outside the home like her mother has had since Jill was born. This expectation isn't considered unusual, and attending college or a technical school to acquire marketable skills is expected.

She helps around the house as does her father and other members of the family. Keeping the house clean and orderly is not the function of her mother alone. The role models of both her father and mother have convinced her that cooperation is essential to growing family relationships.

The car continues to be the means for getting her to and from social engagements as well as for taking the family on vacations. Her introduction to the computer several years ago has made it possible for her to use the one now in the home. The family purchased it for educational purposes and for assisting the father in his work. He goes to the office only twice a week and works in the home the other three days. Her mother's work is still at the office although she, too, has become more dependent upon the home computer.

The family mood is more conservative than it was in the mid-1980s. The parents have attempted to provide a more stable home base for the children as well as for themselves. Discipline and postponing gratification have become important. In addition, her parents have done more things together during the intervening years in order to solidify their relationship. Their efforts have resulted in a more conservative life pattern and a morality that understands but doesn't condone divorce.

Jill is a part of the mix of family, peers, church, and school. Her attitudes have gained direction and maturity as they have been tested against the morals and life patterns of those to whom she is most accountable. She has not been subservient in adapting but has tested the boundaries on behavior set by her parents. Now, in her early teens, she is more certain of her direction and feels that the base upon which her future decisions will be made is solid. She is aware that this is not the condition of many others her age. Broken families have had a demoralizing effect on some of her friends, but for others increased attention from uncles and aunts and grandparents has provided the stability that they needed at critical times.

Jill enjoys the family's portable videotape set. It was purchased to record some of the events that were broadcast while they were on their vacations, but Jill uses it to tape many specials on television when she can't be home to watch them. She is required to watch at least two cable television educational programs each week for school. In one class she can report on either a book or a television program.

This is the background against which we can examine Jill's life in 1990 as she tries to grow up to be a Christian.

Major Social Problems

"My goodness, hasn't she grown! She's becoming a young woman!"

"You're right, Grandma. I had to get some new clothes this week. I've outgrown almost everything in my closet during the last three months."

The early teens, twelve to fourteen years of age, is a time of physical, emotional, and spiritual growth. Physical growth seems to come in spurts. Girls mature before boys and notice physical changes in their bodies that indicate the early stages of womanhood. Boys are slower to mature, but they, too, notice changes that indicate manhood is on the way. Some boys, at this age, will be embarrassed when their voices crack, but this is merely another signal of the onset of maturity.

Psychological growth comes from social contacts. Growth occurs as Jill compares her personal feelings with those reported by her peers. She reads certain kinds of magazines to compare what she likes, wears, and does with the fashions and ideas of her peers. She listens to adults, especially parents and teachers, for attitudes and emotions against which she can test her perceptions and verify her inclinations.

She is a social individual and is very concerned about the attitudes and opinions of others regarding her. She is part of a social milieu and joins clubs and groups mainly because her peers join. On the other hand, she rejects certain kinds of clubs because they are "boring." The critique of "boring" may reflect the attitudes of an intimate friend.

Spiritual growth is often associated with emotional growth. Indeed, the search for purpose and one's place in God's universe is both a spiritual and a psychological trek. For the early teen, spiritual growth comes as the images and ideas of early childhood are tested and replaced. These images must fit with her expanding knowledge of the world and how people react and interact with each other, or the images become useless.

She wants to know answers to tough questions about death and heaven and right and wrong. She may not understand the theological intricacies some denominational confirmation materials want her to learn, but she is interested in how her spiritual world is made up and maintained. She may appear to reject this part of her life, but that is because it is a very private and, for many early teens, a scary part of their lives. She isn't quite ready to think about the ultimates of existence unless forced to because of some catastrophe in her life.

The early teen years can be a very tough time for a young person, especially if she is not on a strong relational footing with peers, parents, and other adults. These are years when it is essential to question authority, to look closely at her personal purpose in life, and to evaluate as well as to question the teachings and actions of the institutions, school and church particularly, that have an important impact on her. Her behavior swings with her moods. At times she may be a model young person while later in the day she can't seem to do anything to please either herself or those around her. Getting a grip on her life is her consuming desire.

Perhaps that's why during these years, young people focus

their attention on others. They are looking for a "significant other" on whom to pattern their lives. This is hero worship with a purpose. They want to retain their dream world of idealism as they move into the more realistic phase of becoming an adult. Emotional highs and lows are their most characteristic behavior. They are contradictory since they resist authority but expect it to help them in testing their own moral development. It is perhaps the most difficult age group to deal with, much less live with.

The child is developing her basis for future life decisions during these early teen years. She will reject or modify early childhood behavior and thought patterns because they represent what older people wanted her to do. With an increasing sense of self identification, the early teen is trying to forge a world view of her own making. Of course she wants someone close by to help pick up the pieces if she should fail. Nevertheless, she wants most desperately to make her own decisions, a trait she will retain in the years ahead.

The major problems for an early teen are personal and take place in a social context. They have to do with sex, living as a family member, trying to communicate her experiences with technology to parents who do not understand nor care about such technology, deciding whether or not to become involved with a foreign substance such as alcohol, tobacco, or drugs, and attempting to handle her life when there is a lack of direction and discipline from parents and other adults. The situations in which she must decide are sometimes overwhelming for her. She needs people to help with the decisions, but mostly she wants others to listen as she verbalizes what she sees as options. She wants others to help her resolve conflicts that each option can bring. She wants affirmation of values that underlie her feelings of right and wrong.

The early teen, because of the intensity of social pressures on her as a person, is not going to get involved for too long a time in issues gnawing at adults. She is only remotely aware of or concerned about global injustice or the threat of nuclear war most of the time. A social problem to her is choosing appropriate clothes to wear so that she will not be out of place with her peers. Her attention is centered on wanting to conform while being her own person. Problems associated with personal and social relationships are crucial to her early-teen life pattern. Her daily decisions about getting along with others, while small and immediate, are, in the long run, life changing.

Sex is a big topic for the early teen of 1990. Jill formed her perceptions of what makes people attractive back in the early 1980s as she watched television and the R-rated movies she attended occasionally with older persons. In addition, her school has a continuing sex-education curricula to which she has been exposed since she was in first grade. To her, sex is a normal part of life.

While sex and attractiveness are normal parts of her life, sexual activity is not an acceptable option for her. A few of her acquaintances experiment with sex, but she and her friends do not. It is not part of her psychology or life pattern to experiment with her body.

Jill's attitudes are in keeping with general societal feelings about sex. Societal feelings about sex and sexual activity have gotten conservative during the late 1980s. While there is no pretense of establishing a sexual code resembling the victorian mode, mores condoning quick and easy sex have been replaced. During the past few years some of the more explicit sex scenes and activities have been cut out of television shows.

Jill is still under some restrictions at home with regard to the types of television shows she may watch and movies she may attend. This is sometimes frustrating to her when at school her friends compare notes on particular movies or shows. However, as they make comparisons, she has discovered that she is not the only one who has guidelines for television viewing. Nearly half of her friends have restrictions as well.

The conserving mood begun in the 1980s has carried into 1990. In addition to concern for energy and environment, there is also a concern for morality in general. The emphasis on personal integrity and care of one's body has increased, and these are now part of the habits of Jill and most of her friends. Living out her intentions is not as easy as she would like it to be, but the conservative mood of society makes decisions regarding sex and morality more narrow than those faced by her friends' sisters only five years ago.

The divorce rate has subsided somewhat during the past few years, but half of her friends are in families in which a divorce has occurred. She has watched these friends struggle with their personal identity because of a shift in family names and living places. She has wondered how she would feel if divorce changed her family. Her apprehensiveness accelerates when she witnesses an argument or fight between her parents, even though she understands that conflict and not getting along all the time are normal. The fact of so many split marriages makes her uneasy.

Another problem she faces with regard to divorce is the attitude some of her friends have toward it. They seem to think that it is a normal part of living. Of course, some of them don't, especially the girls who have had a very difficult time adjusting to a new family situation. She isn't certain that separation is a good thing because it hasn't been part of her family life. She wants to believe that her family is normal and those that are broken are not normal. However, there are so many of her friends coming from broken homes that she isn't quite certain which pattern is normal.

One of the biggest problems in communicating with her parents lies in the different perceptions she and they hold about technology. She understands and can use computers very well. Her parents have a computer in their home now and use it but don't want to experiment with it. She wants to hook up with the national communication network that has become available this year so that they can mail, bank and shop from their home. Of course these services were available five years ago, but they were nowhere near as convenient or widespread as they are now. She thinks her parents are old-fashioned because they don't see the benefits of using the computer for those things.

Her parents and other adults have drilled into her the danger of substance abuse. She has been repeatedly warned of the dangers of alcohol and drugs. She doesn't understand, given their warnings, why her parents drink alcohol at parties in their home. If drinking is not good for one's body, it stands to reason that it shouldn't be used. Her parents are living deceitfully if they think she doesn't know wine is potentially as dangerous as any other form of alcohol. She isn't allowed to drink any alcohol, but their example doesn't help her believe that substance abuse is always harmful.

Maybe it's at the point of being firm and on a straight path that she faults her parents the most. She knows all the family's behavior rules, but her parents treat her like a child. She would like to change these rules to allow for her greater maturity. For example she would like to stay out later than 10:30 P.M. once in a while, but they are very strict about time. On the other hand they are lax on things she considers just as important. For instance, she can't understand why they let her talk back to them and use formerly prohibited language in their presence. She wants to be corrected and is confused and disappointed when they don't correct her. She proposes many things and really wants to do only a few. She wants to sound like an adventurer, but in no way does she want the risk that doing all those things would invite.

How can she get her parents to help her set new boundaries? She doesn't feel she can sit down and make deals with them. Where can she turn to find someone who can tell them her outbursts and arguing and wheedling are ways she has of testing behavior boundaries? She wants limitations, but they must be reasonable and understandable. She wants her parents to help set these and to enforce them even though she may not find the enforcement pleasant all the time. This is a big problem and one she wishes she could deal with adequately.

The problems she faces are important, which makes the solutions critical. She is a social person and turns to others for advice and counsel. It is to these groups and their influence on her that we turn next.

Peer Groups

Jill's friendships have changed dramatically since she has entered junior high school. The number of possible friendships increased geometrically as she moved from elementary school to junior high school because junior high school students were drawn from four elementary schools which encompass half of the community.

She has some constant friends. These friendships reflect long-time associations with several families and include close friends from elementary school. However, peripheral friends from elementary school have been replaced in the early months of attendance at the junior high school. The mix of students in classes and activities has broadened her range of options considerably.

She makes new friends carefully even though she tries to be friendly to most students. She knows friendship is a special form of relationship. Her experience with making changes in friendship groups is typical. Most early teens revise their peer groups dramatically by the end of their first semester in junior high school.

While changes in peer groups are normal, the accompanying personal adjustments are difficult. Her values are tested as she associates with new acquaintances. Her ideas about sex, foreign substance use, and independence need to be revised, reaffirmed, or rejected if she wishes to be part of a particular group. These new friends are not subservient, elementary school children who were afraid of authority and unsure of themselves. They may be uncertain of their personal identity and place in the world, but they display that insecurity in an aggressive manner much of the time. Even though she may take on some of the unpleasant attributes of her age, she tends to choose friends who act and believe as she does. Her social world must reflect her basic values.

Being part of a circle of friends is necessary. Having several members in a friendship clique allows her to move from "best friend" to "best friend" within the group. The larger group gives her a support base and still opens the possibilities of selecting close friends when she needs certain kinds of help. In addition, the friendship circle gives her access to other groups because each member of a group has ties and is part of one or more other friendship circles.

Her friendship clique consists of half a dozen people. These peers she considers to be close friends but she tends to trust and confide in no more than two. She competes with her friendship clique in academic as well as in other activities. She has developed a special trust with them and can predict their actions and feelings quite well. Perhaps one of them has been her friend during elementary school. These people are her peer group and provide a basis for her decision making about dress, relationships, and general behavior.

Her perceptiveness of what her friends do for and to her may not be the same as her parents' observations and evaluations of them. In fact, the group of friends Jill chooses in the early months of junior high school may be a controversial subject at home. The reason for this difference is the change in the kind of social group Jill needs at this time. She is beginning to break the strong ties with home and replace them cautiously with peer friendships. At this time, the parents and adults in general, tend to be of a different social world. Jill must learn to relate in her world, which means choosing and associating with her peers.

This is difficult for parents to accept. They know the impressionableness of the early teen years. They are interested in keeping their child more dependent than independent. The aggressiveness of the early teen as well as her penchant for talking back and openly expressing moods become difficult for parents to understand or accept. They often feel like they have lost a daughter as she denounces a value which her parents feel is quite important. The parents must be aware that denouncing is one of her means of testing as are her critical comments about the way the family gets along.

Recognizing this age as one of emerging independence, questioning, and trying to adapt to new social demands from her peers is critical for Jill's parents. They are needed more now than previously, although they are needed in a different way. Parents must become counselors and exert strong discipline tempered with the kind of love that encourages growth and responsibility in the young person. Of most importance to the early teen is advice from parents as she selects from among the many possible activities in which she can become involved. She needs guidance to choose those activities that can do the most to help her develop her own skills and personality while keeping her life centered on Christian values.

Selecting Activities

Friends are important to the early teen because they are part of the activities in which she participates. Her participation in activities will help her to express talents, interests, and values. Her activities during elementary school were determined for her. Now, in junior high school, she must choose from a wide vista of activities that is spread before her. She will be confused and overwhelmed by this array at first. Having to choose among the many alternatives will be intimidating. She will need help to make good decisions. She will discover that she makes some mistakes in decision making. Making the wrong decision is a constant worry.

The freedom of making choices in the junior high school includes resisting her parents' insistence that she be involved in particular kinds of activities. She can choose new areas of interest. Instead of music she can choose sports. Instead of sports she can choose drama. The critical difference between elementary and junior high school is that the choice of what activities to become involved in is hers. From now on her parents will be one among several groups from which she wants approval. In addition to her parents, her peers and teachers become important counselors.

The activities from which she will need to choose are clubs related to junior high school, social or community-wide groups, special interests such as drama, and those offered to early teens by the church. Age thirteen is an important milestone because opportunities that had not been available now open up. More competitive sports are available to students in junior high school. No longer is the young athlete competing against just other neighborhood persons. Teams from other communities are on the docket. These "outside" teams bring different life-styles and values into their games. This tentative clash of life patterns makes the early teen test assumptions and attitudes as she competes.

Special interest groups include music, drama, art, and outdoor adventure. Being a member of a band or an orchestra that draws members from a county rather than a community is a new possibility. Participating in a community drama club or group becomes possible as does taking lessons from the local art center. These special interest opportunities expand her vision and acquaint the early teen with the diffuse cultural desires and traditions of those around her. She will be protected in her contacts, but when dealing with peers from other communities, she will have to assert her own value system against theirs. It is in these interchanges among early teens from the wider community that much testing of personal beliefs and morals is conducted.

In addition to opening new contacts with different kinds of people, this plethora of activities puts new pressure upon Jill. She must choose from several equally appealing activities because there is not enough time to be involved in all of them. Her choices may be affected by the scheduling of activities in which she wants to participate. It is impossible to be in more than one place at a time. Thus if the drama club and computer club meet Wednesday after school and the church choir practices at the same time, she must choose one of the three possibilities.

Her choices among activities are affected by several influences. One influence is her personal interest. This is powerful, and by the early teen years she has begun to think of the long-term effect of pursuing an interest. Her school counselors have begun to tell her about life work and now her interests and skills may eventuate in a career or hobby. This is part of her decision process as she chooses from alternatives.

Another influence is the peer group, her friends. They do not have as much influence on Jill's choice of activities as they do on her attitudes about clothes and social involvements with other people, especially boys in Jill's case. Jill is more independent of her peer's judgments with regard to her choice of activities even though she might be inclined to think about doing some of the same things they do. She asserts her independence from peers even as she wants their approval of her choices.

Her parents can be quite influential in her choice of activities if they help her to evaluate the long-term consequences of her choices. Those parents who can assist without making choices for an early teen are very valuable. When parents tell a young person what he or she should do, it is possible that the early teenager will make that choice but will handle it only averagely or poorly. The most helpful parental role is that of advising and helping the early teen weigh the benefits to herself of participating in one of several attractive possibilities. Equally important is providing support when a wrong choice is made. Assisting the early teenager to evaluate experiences is a valuable contribution parents can make.

The church has an influence on her choices because it often offers several possible activities for the early teen. The church is seen as a peer group by the early teen. She sees those who will be participating with her and gauges her relationship to them as being as strong or stronger or weaker than her ties to those who will be involved with her in activities outside the church. Of major importance is the teacher or leader of the choir or youth group to which the early teen might belong. The caliber and attitude of the adult leaders are crucial determining factors on whether or not the early teen chooses the church's activities as opposed to other kinds of activities.

Selecting activities is very important to the early teen. Deciding not to participate in any activity is an important decision. She will not be alone since many other early teens will make the same decision. Without the social engagement that activities afford and the support of a larger peer group, she tends to function as a social isolate. As such, she will become more open to sexual experimentation and foreign substance use than her peers who are involved in various types of organized activities. Her energies will not be directed or channeled as are the energies of those who participate in organized clubs and activities. Without the direction that organized activities provide, the early teen may drift into groups that are antisocial. On the other hand, the early teen who decides not to participate in activities may find outlets in an after-school job or in a hobby that does not require the involvement of others. Computers is one such activity.

It is impossible to be an early teen and not make a decision about participating in some sort of activity. This is not an age of guietude. It is an active, exploring, testing age. The question for Jill, her parents, and the church is what kind of activities are best suited to express a growing Christian's life pattern? The importance of the impact others have in helping her answer this question is our next concern.

Significant Others

Adults are more important than peers when it comes to an early teenager's decisions about life choices and patterns. Adults set the boundaries, make the rules, and evaluate the performances of the early teen. The young person may resist the authority of adults and test the boundaries that they set, but in the final anaylsis adults will be in control. That is a fact of life for an early teen.

Some adults are more important than others. It doesn't take long to determine which teacher, for instance, is considered more important. Nicknames tell the story. "Monkey face," "fat Gert," "Mad Mel," and other tags give parents an idea of which teachers are less than influential in the decision-making process of the early teen. The nicknames do not address the importance of the teachers in their subject matter. The nicknames apply to the personality and real influence of the teachers on the learners.

A "significant other" is a person, usually an adult, whose attitudes and living pattern become a model for an early teen. This person may be a parent, a teacher, a clergyperson, a relative, or a friend of the family. A certain amount of idealization by the teen is part of the image of a significant other and makes his or her subsequent influence strong. An early teen will try to live according to the example set by the significant other. This involves translating the image into reality, as this is perceived by a thirteen year old, and may not be fully recognizable to parents or the significant other.

It is possible that an early teen will have two or three adults who serve as significant others. It then becomes important for her or him to choose the best traits of each and combine them in her or his behavior patterns. It is not the skill or ability of the significant other that is being emulated. The teen is emulating the significant other's attitudes and living pattern. Of great importance is the way the adult listens and reacts to the early teen. If the adult treats the early teen as an individual with something to say and appreciate his or her abilities, it is likely that what that adult says and does will be quite influential to the early teen.

This doesn't mean that a significant other is a friend like a peer group member. An early teen doesn't need an adult as a peer. An early teen wants an adult to be an adult but one who considers her or him worthy of being listened to carefully. The early teen wants, like persons of every age, to be treated as an individual whose ideas and suggestions make a difference in the way things are done. This is critical for adult church leaders to understand. Applying discipline, giving directions, and planning meetings are expected activities of adults. Early teenagers know they don't have those skills yet. What they most desire is contacts with adults who listen to them and demonstrate that their insights make a difference. However, early teenagers aren't interested in an adult who does only what the teens want to do. That becomes boring.

A significant other is an important and necessary person for the early teen. When adults fail to be role models, the early teen turns to someone else, usually an individual who is just a few years older. This may prove to be a disaster and is often the first step toward a career as a juvenile delinquent. People need a hero, which is another name for a significant other. Early teen experience is limited to those close to them. They will choose a hero and try their best to live like that person. Providing a good role model, being a positive significant other, is an obligation as well as an opportunity for the adults who care about the early teen. This opportunity should not be lost by the church.

Community

People are social entities and live in social environments. An early teen tends to absorb the general social attitudes and morality of the community. While the community environment may not be finally determinative of the life pattern of an early teen, it will leave an impact. This influence will be noticed in the early teen's feelings about school, about family life, about a career, about authority, about abiding by social constraints, and most everything else in a social environment.

In 1990 the community in which many early teens will be growing up will be media conscious. The computer will be an important instrument in banking, mail service, and communications. It will record and store the early teen's grades, aptitude scores from tests, and involvement in school as it tracks her participation not only in academic but in social and school activities. Its widespread use will be accepted as a normal part of life, and most early teens will be using it at school in some aspect of learning.

Family life will have become more stable with fewer divorces. However, by 1990 nearly half of the families of early teens will have been affected by divorce. This will have created problems of adjustment for many young people as they have had to learn to get along with more than two parents and must give their allegiance to extended families. Their support base may not be as stable as they need during those times when conflicts with peers leave them vulnerable. In addition, the mixture of families may have created a mixture of values and life patterns that the early teen finds confusing.

The emphasis in the community on conserving, noticed during the late 1970s and early 1980s has increased. For example, in some nearby towns it is required by law that newspapers and metals be separated from garbage and placed at the curbside on certain days for special collection. These communities sell the newspapers and metals for recycling. The installation of new kinds of lights for public streets and buildings and an emphasis on turning off lights is part of the increased emphasis on energy conservation. Water use is controlled, during the summer especially, since water is an important and scarce commodity.

The community has increased its recreational facilities and improved its early teen sports programs. Now it is possible for girls to compete in organized sports. In fact, as many girls are enrolled on town softball and soccer teams as are boys. Tennis courts, outdoor exercise and hiking trails, and parks have been added during the past five years. It seems as though the desire of the community is to keep people active rather than to allow them to sit passively before the television.

Crime has decreased somewhat because the most frequent offenders have grown older and tend not to be included in crime any longer. Even so, the early teen is taught to be careful of those who are dealers and users of foreign substances. The problem of drinking is prevalent especially among older brothers and sisters of early teenagers. They got involved with alcohol when they were early teens and have had a hard time breaking the habit.

Adults, including Jill's parents, continue to further their education through community supported schools. Taking courses in computer and art has been an important activity for her mother while courses in computer and gardening have occupied her father. In addition, both of her parents follow a schedule of personal exercise. Once in a while they go to the school gym to participate in a specific exerise program.

Traveling remains a part of Jill's environment. People in the community have traveled all over the world. They have stories to tell and are candid in evaluating the cultures of other countries. They are not hesitant to point out the shortcomings of their own nation and community. This information has produced a positive feeling about the various cultures that are represented among the townspeople. In fact, some refugees from the Middle East as well as Central America have found new homes in Jill's community. While in the community are those who dislike any newcomers, the general attitude has been one of acceptance.

Jill, as an early teen in 1990, has absorbed many of these attitudes: conservatism, exercise is essential, learning is lifelong, and accepting people whose cultures are different from hers. Other communities have resisted these perspectives and have a negative attitude about life. Jill has discovered that her peers in these communities are more apathetic and tend to be distrustful of her life pattern. She is sometimes frightened by their hostility toward her because she has done nothing to them. She tries but finds it impossible to understand their way of life or thinking.

The church, as part of the larger community, seeks to provide Jill with a more narrow definition of values and life pattern than is found in general community attitudes. In doing so, it must perform its roles well and consistently. It is to these roles that we turn.

The Church's Role

Being an early adolescent in the church sometimes means being lost in the crevice between children's and youth pro-

gramming. Since early adolescence is an age of transition between elementary and high school years, adults often feel that
it is a less important age than those before and after. In addition,
this age group is so difficult to deal with that many adults want
no responsibility for it. Early teens are unpredictable and hard
to manage, have a short attention span, and must be continually
active. They wear out adults with just their energy level.

However, it is at this age that young people make up their
minds about future involvement in the church. They cannot
openly make a break now, but unless the church pays attention
to them and is interested in them, they will decide that church
isn't worth their time. Sometime during high school, when they
feel they can make the break with little opposition from their
parents, they will drop out. While church leaders decry the
dropout rate among high school students, that isn't the time
when they made their decision to quit the church. They made
the decision during their early teen years.

The church is strong in 1990, having survived the hard times
of the 1970s and early 1980s. A general emphasis upon the
search for meaning and a desire to have a strong, stable life
base have combined to encourage people to look to the church
for help. Clergy, meanwhile, have become interested in pursuing a spiritual discipline that reflects itself in solid preaching
and teaching. Activities offered by most congregations for early
teenagers include at least a choir and a fellowship and learning
group. A few congregations have a drama group, a bell choir,
and a camping program. Most congregations, however, rely
upon the Sunday morning church school sessions to keep early
adolescents active and involved.

Early adolescents need, from the church, affirmation in a
value base. They are being tested and buffeted by conflicting
ideas and claims from their peers. They want to know why
their church is important and how it came to be different from
others. More important, they want to know its basic beliefs on
relationships with others, what forgiveness means, how one
expresses love, the boundaries of fidelity, and other life-di-
recting values. They don't want the intricacies of theological
debate, but they do need the opportunity to question and clarify
what is taught so that it becomes part of their values.

These young people also need people from the church to be role models. The role model may be of either sex. The task of these persons is to demonstrate beliefs in action. The early adolescent must see how beliefs are worked out in persons' lives in order to translate abstract beliefs into a useful value base for themselves.

The significant other from the church is indispensable. Such a person may be the choir director, drama coach, school teacher who is a member of the congregation, a clergyperson, or any other member. The critical factor is that the person be actively involved in the church.

The church must also provide opportunities for the early adolescent to test theories. This happens in the fellowship group but becomes more intense and meaningful in drama or musical productions. Camping and retreats are other areas in which testing can be done. Without the opportunity to test ideas about relationships, the values preached by teachers and leaders at church will be abstractions with no meaning to early adolescents.

Young people want as much help as they can get as they live through the early adolescent years. They want this help to be free of oppression. They would like it to be unstructured and not related to discipline. However, they perceive the church to be a structured and disciplined organization. They expect of it a value system that will guide them through whatever difficult times they may face. Mostly they want the church to be a place where they can find peers and leaders who care for them and express concern for others. These are important dimensions of early adolescence that are not addressed regularly any place other than in the church.

This time of transition is crucial to the early teenager as well as to the church. They need each other: the church needs the vitality, questioning, and testing of the young people; the young people need the promise of stability that the church represents. How effectively the church fulfills its roles of helping early adolescents create a strong value base, of providing significant others on which young lives can be modeled, and of endeavoring to structure opportunities for testing and learning to occur will determine whether or not the church has a chance to work with Jill as she reaches her next major milestone. That comes as she graduates from high school. For Jill this will be in 1995. We now turn to this time.

FOUR

Late Teen
Pressures in 1995

"What do you plan to do after you graduate from high school, Jill?"

"I'll probably go to college. I'm very interested in biogenetics and might take a crack at that. My counselor says I'm too people oriented to do that kind of research, but right now that's where my interest is."

"Why would you be interested in biogenetics? Those people think they're God. They're always experimenting with life. I don't like that!"

"I figure somebody with a religious background like me has to be involved in biogenetics just because of that. Ethics have to be a part of those experiments and investigations. People can't take God's place, but we ought to be able to help improve God's creation."

"I never thought of it like that. You make sense to me."

Jill is eighteen in 1995. Her world is very different from that imagined world a decade or two ago. Her parents have roots that extend to midcentury and have seen how quickly the social world has changed in those years. They have been part of the panic of trade boycotts that resulted in the oil embargo of the 1970s and steel controversies of the 1980s. Job and personal habits were greatly affected by the constriction on energy supplies and the internationalization of the steel industry.

International terrorists have been constant menaces over the years. Their escapades have resulted in increased security measures at most public buildings and in airports. People have accepted the inconveniences of security devices as a price of free movement.

Her parents have felt the pinch of inflation in their incomes. They have understood the bleakness of unemployment; her father was without a job for nearly six months. They have struggled through the trauma of role changes; both of the parents worked. The home life Jill experiences now has become more cooperative and understanding since each member of the family must be a working part of the whole. Even visits to the grandparents must be planned around the work and vacation schedules of the parents.

Many changes have come about because of inventions and discoveries made during the past decade. After several years of testing, drugs to cure the common cold, to treat effectively certain forms of cancer, and to influence growth in children with the disease that inhibited growth have become commonplace. Biogenetics, the profession toward which Jill is looking, has found ways to select genes in humans that can eliminate certain birth defects. The biogenetic industry is testing its gene mutation techniques now in human situations.

Jill's house has undergone changes because of products introduced during the past decade. For example, the family has installed a new kind of heating unit that uses solar energy as the catalyst for producing heat in the winter and for running the air conditioning system during the summer. A new type of siding material for houses has been developed to increase the effectiveness of insulation. Room lighting is controlled by sensors that are activated by a person's coming into or leaving a room. The adage "turn off the lights" has been taken care of by this technology. Of course it is still possible to turn off lights in a room manually, but in Jill's house these switches are seldom used.

The household computer of 1990 has been replaced by two more powerful units. These computers have become an integral part of Jill's home life. The computers are programmed to control the heat, answer the telephone when no one is home, monitor the weather and water the lawn when needed, and maintain a security system for the property. In addition to these home chores, one of the computers is attached to a national communication network that allows family members, if they wish to use it, to transfer payments from their bank to the utility companies and most of the stores from which they make purchases. They have used these electronics most frequently to pay insurance premiums although Jill's father occasionally sends electronic mail messages to other offices.

An important change has taken place in shopping malls. Going to the mall has become a significant part of Jill's leisure time. At one of the malls that were constructed during the 1980s around her community, she shops for food, enjoys entertainment at the theater, meets friends for a visit and a snack, and, occasionally, takes a course at the college extension center located there. While shopping malls have much the same products to offer as they did a decade ago, their appearances are quite different. Most of them have been enclosed. The interior parklike area has become a favorite meeting place where older folks and young people can relax and visit. The crime-ridden malls of the 1980s have been made more crime free and, as a result, have become leisure centers in most communities.

More stores have been added in the last decade. The large department stores have been divided into separate stores, each of which appeals to a distinct taste, life pattern, or age group. An important decision for Jill and others is which mall rather than which store do they wish to visit since each mall has a distinct personality and offers a distinct style of merchandise.

These are physical changes that affect social life in 1995. Other changes have created a new social atmosphere. One of the most significant of these is the degree of equality witnessed in society. Women and men receive equal employment opportunities and equal pay, with the consequence that more men are unemployed or choose to stay at home than was true in the 1980s. Equality is a continuing struggle, however. It is possible only because groups that feel they have been deprived of equal justice have won major court battles to secure their rights and continue to enjoin those decisions.

Mobility, especially in the form of immigrants, has influenced many communities including Jill's. These immigrants have come

to the United States looking for freedom and opportunity. Jill
has noticed the influence of immigrant children at school. Many
of her classmates speak two languages because they have moved
into the community from another country. Spanish is most
frequently the second language of her immigrant friends. Most
of their parents are professionals from Central and South America who have come to the United States, looking for a more
stable social situation in which to raise their children. These
friends travel home to their native lands at least once and
sometimes twice a year.

Another important group of classmates has come from the
Far East. They are very competitive and work much harder at
their studies than Jill or her native born classmates. Asian
immigrants are evident in the business and medical parts of
the community. They tend to be hard working and better off
economically than Jill's family. Jill's classmates travel to visit
relatives in their home country annually, but they stay a month
or so when they go.

The changes in the makeup of her class took place gradually.
When she began high school, only a couple of foreign-born
students were in her class. Now, as she prepares to graduate,
more than 10 percent of her classmates were born in other
countries. The primary reason for this increase has been a new
immigration policy affecting the number of people immigrating
from other than European nations. As a result her school, during
the past five years, has become more cosmopolitan. Some of
the prejudices regarding Spanish-speaking and Asian persons
have been revised but have not been eliminated. The school
system is meeting a need rather than being fashionable when
it offers a second language now.

Another significant change has been the increase in the number of single persons. Jill has noticed this in her neighborhood.
The house across the street is owned by two young women
while the one two doors down from her contains two elderly
brothers. She remembers that when she was eight, both houses
were occupied by families. She recalls, as well, the anxiety of
her parents when the two women were looking at the home in
their neighborhood. Her parents feared that the women would
be transient and would not take care of the property. Her parents

were wrong, and the two women, who both work full time and do not intend to marry, have been good neighbors. Their life goals are different from most other residents, but this doesn't seem to bother anyone so much anymore. In fact, diversity has come to be expected.

The efforts of Jill to understand and appreciate life patterns different from her own have not always been successful. She continues to hold to values and attitudes that have been implanted by her church and family during the intervening decade. She believes in fidelity, wants to be careful of her body and mind, desires to be useful to others in her life work, and is willing to live conservatively regarding the environment. However these are general precepts that affect but may not guide every minute decision she makes.

It's easy for us who live in the mid-1980s to know what she should do and how she should choose. However, we haven't been part of the monumental changes of that decade. Jill, however, has been part of these changes and has absorbed them as a part of her maturation. She is aware of the changes in the energy system and in lighting devices in her home. She has heard about but not used the new international money. She knows about the increase of single persons by the people living in her neighborhood. She has come face-to-face with the increasing diversity in population at school. Being aware of social changes is not the same as understanding their impact on her future decisions. After all, she has been protected by the school and her family during this decade.

We can only hope that her youthful experiences have prepared her for the giant steps she is about to take. As she graduates from high school, she is completing one phase of life and beginning a new one. The strength of her faith and values in addition to the adequacy of her training will be tested during the next few months and years. We want to understand some of the dynamics playing on her and influencing her decisions. In particular, we want to know how the church can help her during the next few months of life-shaping choices.

What's After High School?

Jill's counselors in high school, her parents, and her peers have been talking to her about life beyond high school for the past two years. She has taken aptitude tests, has looked at career possibilities, and has taken the battery of scholastic tests that are used partly for determining eligibility to graduate and partly for applying to colleges she might want to attend. She has been presented with career options at the church by the youth group leader even though she hasn't regularly attended the youth program this past year. The youth leader made it a point to bring her a booklet of opportunities for careers in the church. In addition, she has received information about government service, which is expected of high school graduates although it is not yet mandatory.

She is not left alone to make a decision. She is inundated with information and possibilities. She is very much aware that she has reached a new phase of her life. She hasn't suddenly become mature although the choices she must make in the next few weeks and months will be hard to change as she grows older. Her support system of friends and peers will certainly be different and the emotional ties she has had with them will be replaced by new friends. She is more confused than helped by the good intentioned advice and counsel everyone is offering her. She is frightened by the deadlines that govern her decision making. Pressures she feels from every quarter are intense. She has not been prepared for the immediacy of the demands. Yet, when she shares her frustration with adults, they only nod and agree that choices are difficult and deadlines are impossible. They are no help!

The most important realization she has come to during the last weeks of high school is that her protected days will be gone. She is being treated as an adult and is required to make decisions with long-term consequences. Her consolation is that her peers are making the same kinds of choices. It is important for her to share her frustrations and hopes with them and to listen to their plans. This interchange with others her own age helps to relieve some of her anxiety. Yet, as she thinks and tries to visualize her new life, she begins to understand no one else can make up her mind for her. The day of reckoning is here.

In her mind she looks at the future as an extension of her present. She wants to pursue her interests which, at this time, are in the area of biogenetics. She is intrigued with the possibilities of finding cures for genetic diseases. She feels she can make a contribution to others by being in this field.

On the other hand, she likes the freedom that the money from her part-time job has given her during the past year. Her employer has offered her a full-time position if she wants to work for the next couple of years. It is tempting to consider the options she would enjoy with the money she could earn. If she wanted to go to college in two years, she would have money enough to pay her own way. She would have enough money to do some traveling and perhaps to afford a small automobile. However, the negative side of working two years would be the postponement of the start of her real career. Her parents caution that she might not get started if she waits two years. She isn't totally convinced by their argument, but it makes enough sense to consider.

While she isn't serious about getting married right away, she knows several classmates who intend to marry as soon as they graduate. She wants to postpone getting serious with anyone until she's at least twenty-five. That's seven years away, and a person can't really predict what will happen in that length of time. What if she should get serious with someone in her home town during the next two years? How would she handle it? Could she make a break and go away to school? After all, she wants the career.

A concern of her parents, although not expressed to her, is a possible pregnancy. She hasn't been involved in sexual activity although she has dated often. Her morality just doesn't include intimate sexual relations. Some of her acquaintances have relationships in which they regularly use birth control methods, but she is not aware of any of her friends who do. Her friendship clique doesn't condone that sort of thing. She knows at least half a dozen classmates who have given birth during their high school days. Usually the babies have been given up for adoption, and the girls have returned to school.

Separating from her group is most on her mind. As she looks at the places where she would like to go to school, she discovers that she must go alone. No one else in her group is interested in biogenetics. While that doesn't surprise her, she is frightened by the need to go to a school where she would have no support group. Even though everyone tells her making friends will be easy, she isn't willing to think about breaking off with her close associates. No other group would be the same to her. She has had such good times and shared so much with these girls that she feels no one can take their places. This feeling is an important influence in her procrastination in making a decision about what she is going to do next.

Withdrawing into herself is not possible, however. People are pressuring her to make decisions. Only during the last three months of school has she finally been able to decide. Her friends have been accepted at colleges or have made agreements with employers. She and a few others haven't decided. One day she spontaneously decides. Of course, her decision has been carefully considered and talked over often with peers, parents, and others. It only appears spontaneous to her. She has really run out of time and has been forced to choose. What she is remotely aware of is that she must live out the decision. She will feel the implications of her choice for the rest of her life.

Adults may feel that a decision about a life pattern made by an eighteen year old can be changed easily. It can't. In the first place, it takes a great deal of thought and emotional energy to make a choice at a time when a very important phase of one's life is ending. That's what is happening with Jill when high school ends. The group to which Jill belongs has been held together by a common schedule and enforced work pattern. Both of these conditions are eliminated at graduation, and the group members will be forced apart by their own interests and needs. Jill may never see some of them again, and she knows it. In a real sense her world is breaking up with the same finality that it did when she entered junior high school.

Jill is being forced to participate in an adult world in which she is a minor citizen. She has no history with these people. She can't compete on their level because she doesn't know the rules of their game. She is regarded an an interloper by some and strong competition by others. She is uncomfortable. This world, composed of her parents' associates and friends, doesn't appear at all friendly or helpful. Her protection is stripped away, and she feels awkward and insecure.

When she needs help, she isn't certain where to turn. She must depend upon her own intuition to lead her to people who care about her and who can give her advice with which she can live. The influence of these people on her life pattern will be crucial. Who they are makes all the difference.

Influences on Decision Making

When she's eighteen, the group to which Jill goes for advice when making a decision has changed considerably from the group she depended on five years earlier. Now she relies on her parents, two other adults, her expectations of herself, and her self-image that was created during high school. Her self-image has been nurtured by her friendship clique that helped her to develop it. This image includes personal integrity, interests, ability to make friends easily, and the attitudes she expresses on most everything. While the image is her own, it is a product of her interaction with her friends and associates at school.

Being liked is very important to Jill. When she is liked, she can function well with others. When someone doesn't overtly express or give positive body language to Jill, she feels uncomfortable. Insecurity is a constant companion of eighteen year olds. It is accentuated by feeling uncomfortable. Jill tries to be in social situations where her image is appreciated and in which she can feel comfortable. Making her feel at ease is the major contribution of her peer group. In this sense, it is an influential part of her decision-making process. Having the group around when she wants to discuss her future options is important, but she is not willing to be guided totally by the group's opinions.

Jill's own personal interests are her most influential guide for decision making at eighteen. Her problem is narrowing choices down to one interest from among the many that excite her. Jill has spent the past couple of years trying to focus her sights on a particular area in which she can develop a career. By the time she has graduated from high school, that area has become biogenetics. She has committed herself to this choice in conversations and through choices of high school subjects. Her decision doesn't mean that she will spend the remainder of her life as a biogeneticist. She knows her interest in biogenetics may be camouflaging a more basic desire in some other field. Yet she must choose, and her interest now is biogenetics.

Jill's parents have become very influential in her choices at this time. Until now school authorities and counselors pretty much guided Jill's choices. They can't anymore. Fortunately, Jill has maintained a good relationship with her parents. She is saddened by the problems some of her friends have in finding adults to help with decision making. Most of them, because their homes have not been as stable as hers, must find adults other than their parents in whom to confide, or they are forced to depend on their peer group. They tend to take the road of least resistance and to do whatever the adult or peer group says. Jill, however, turns to her parents to discuss options.

The most important concern of her parents is to encourage Jill toward a career. They point out that women must be independent and be able to provide for themselves. They caution her to postpone any commitments for marriage until she has settled on a career and completed preparation for entering it. They point to the women across the street as examples of the need to be independent. They urge her not to think that marriage will relieve her of responsibility for life's obligations. They had suggested that she consider a field that would allow her freedom to move from one to another speciality such as research, management, or retail. She and they feel that biogenetics offers such an option.

In the final analysis, her parents' suggestions make much sense, and Jill feels comfortable with her choices. She can take this choice to the church and test it with the youth leader and her peers there, but the choice has been made. It becomes a topic of conversation from this point forward. Once this choice is made; the place where she will go for further schooling is also chosen. Now she feels a bit more comfortable about life. However, this feeling will not last long. During the next few weeks she must face her decision anew. During the time between high school graduation and her entrance on a career, she will continually need to verify her choice.

Implications of Jill's Decision

Any choice Jill makes about her life eliminates other choices. Thus each decision creates both opportunities and limitations.

Selecting between opportunities doesn't seem as though it should curtail other options, but, in a social setting, that is what happens. A choice carries with it an investment of Jill's social image. She may not feel as committed to the choice as her friends think she is. However, when she must explain and defend her decision, her commitment grows. In addition, her social standing and status among her peers and in other groups are automatically related to her choice.

In this way, a decision contains its own set of implications. The most important implication of Jill's selection is the peer group to which she will belong. If her decision is to work for the summer and attend college or trade school in the fall, the peer group at work is temporary. She and they acknowledge its impermanence and act accordingly. However, if she had decided to work full time, the peer group at her job would have tested and initiated her as a member. In the fall when she becomes a student, she will join a student body peer group that has its mortality built in.

When she joins a peer group, she must pass its tests of acceptance. These tests will determine her social position. Groups test new members by relegating them to the lowest social category. This means, on the job, doing the undesirable work for the group, such as doing the final cleanup for the day, running errands, and standing in line to get snacks for other members at break time. Ridiculing and making jokes about his or her appearance and work are other ways a peer group tests a new member. The reactions of the new member and the discomfort she or he expresses during the testing will help the group to assign her or him to a position. This initial placement is hard to break out of even when an individual leaves the group.

It makes little difference if the new peer group is at work or at school, Jill must successfully complete her tests before being accepted. Her salvation at school is that she is one among many other neophytes who are undergoing testing at the same time. She gains support from her fellow sufferers and thus quickly builds a peer group from among them. Her dormitory room assignment will prove to be another test especially if the roommate is an upperclass student.

The difference between her reaction to this new peer group

at college and her reaction to those with which she associated in the past is her recognition of this group as temporary. The members change often, sometimes each semester and most assuredly each year. As a result, she will feel the influence of this peer group mostly in her decisions about social activities. It can have long-term influences on her life pattern. Members of this peer group will discuss life-changing as well as more immediate issues related to courses and current friendships. She will find the new peer group to be very important.

Other factors in her decision to attend college will change her life pattern completely. Perhaps the most important of these is the selection of a college which will require that she live away from home. Of course many college students, including some of Jill's friends, live at home for at least part of their student life, and many young adults who work live at home as well. However, in Jill's instance, her decision includes moving to a dormitory at her new school.

The physical separation from home forces Jill to leave a protected environment. Once she is away from this setting, she must create the surroundings, including choosing friends, that will support her life values and life pattern. Her first efforts, are focused on finding appropriate friends, a new peer group. She may change friends several times during the first few months but usually will fall in with a group whose values either reflect or are close to those she holds.

This venture away from home involves major testing of her values and life pattern. Her decision to leave home and go away to school implies that she is willing to pit her values and life pattern against the life pattern and values of others with whom she will live. The support she receives from her family is very important during the first few months in her new setting because their values and life pattern become the peg to which she can hold during trying times. If she had no stable family, she would no doubt turn to another significant adult or reference group that have become substitute parents. She may not have foreseen that testing of life patterns and values were part of her decision to attend college away from home, but this is what happens. If she had decided to stay at home to attend school or work, her testing would have occurred, but it would have been done as she lived in a more protected setting.

The choice of attending school also implies that Jill is choosing a particular kind of career. Even if pursuing a career had been a fuzzy idea during high school, her decision to go away to school created the image that her commitment to a career has been made. A reversal of her choice to have a career will be hard for her and her former peer group to accept. She will need to forge a new social image and develop a new peer group if she drops out of school.

Her selection of biogenetics as her career goal can be changed during her schooling with few negative repercussions. When she shifts her course of study, however, the student peer group to which she has related in her former field of study will change as well. She will join another group in her new area of concentration. In this way her associations with other students are affected by a new career option, but redirecting an area of study is a normal part of college. She will not change her primary peer group even though she will make new acquaintances and friends among those in the new career path.

In addition to establishing a new peer group, testing her life pattern and values, creating a support base, and deciding on a career, Jill, by her decision to attend college away from home, has set parameters for a marriage partner if she chooses to marry. This partner must be accepting of her career ambitions, be supportive of her life pattern, and be able to share the responsibilities of life with her. While none of these may be foremost in her mind when she chooses to go to school, they are implications of that decision.

Influences Affecting Jill

Jill will adapt her life pattern while she is in college because of new influences in her life. Freedom to follow her own interests with limited interference from her family is both frightening and exhilarating. She can do things now that she was forbidden to do previously including traveling by herself, purchasing alcohol for consumption, attending certain kinds of movies and shows, and living with someone other than a parent. She has seen these options from afar and has known girls her age who did these things while in high school. But her values and parents would not allow her to do any of them. Now she has to choose whether or not to do them.

The peer group she selects will have much influence on what she does. Her friends tend to reflect her values and life patterns but they also are at the age of experimentation. It is possible for Jill to have the same set of values she has held for years and, with her new friends, to experiment with different values. She does this by trying new things. In fact, it is likely that this will happen. She must either experience alternative life patterns or be convinced by observation of others that her choice of life pattern is correct. This testing occurs with the support of a peer group and usually in association with a close friend.

That's the reason her choice of peers when she moves away from home or takes a job is so important. They will be guiding her in social decisions and attitudes that will affect her life permanently. Testing and experimenting with her life pattern's values give her a basis for choosing her life-style from among those that are available. Her peer group, even if it is temporary, will have tremendous influence on her because the values and life pattern she forms during the next four or five years will be hard to break in later life. Making these decisions at eighteen is hard but inevitable.

Parents remain a key influence group for Jill. While she may not acknowledge their importance, it is their values and teachings that she is testing. She will need to revise their pattern so that the one she makes will fit her interests and goals. Jill may not tell her parents how much influence they have on her because she may not realize it herself.

An obvious area of influence of her parents is Jill's choice of college and where she will live. While they can't choose her new friends, they can help her find a place where her basic values are upheld. They can help her select a school in which she has a supportive base as she builds her life away from the confines of her home.

The community to which she moves will be influential on her selection of a life pattern. If the school is located in a metropolitan area, her choices of a life-style may be limited to the confines of the university, or she may be influenced by any of the number of life-styles evident in the city. If her school is located in a smaller community in which the college is a major industry, it is likely that the atmosphere and morality of the school will limit her choices of life-style. If she chooses to live in an apartment rather than a dormitory, her choice of life pattern is wider. The surroundings provided by the community in which she locates will encourage particular types of life patterns.

This community influence is seen in the kinds of entertainment, culture, and jobs of which Jill can take advantage. Her attitudes toward the community will reflect a comparison of it with her home town. If there are many advantages for Jill to grow and learn and she participates in community affairs, its influence will be positive. If she focuses her attention on her school and looks at the community as off limits or uninteresting, its influence will be negative.

Another important influence on Jill comes from her "significant others," adults who mean a lot to her. She needs their care and support as she proceeds through the testing that is part of college experiences. She must have open communication with them. Her insecurity may inhibit her from making the first contact, but if contact comes from the others, she will welcome it. She is seeking their willingness to listen to her abundance of problems and dilemmas. In addition she wants their advice but doesn't need guilt trips.

When one or more of those significant others are part of her hometown church, that is so much the better. The church in Jill's life as an eighteen year old can and should be very important.

The Church's Role

"Out of sight, out of mind" is the way many congregations view young people who go away from home after high school graduation. For some unexplainable reason, congregations feel that their obligation to the young person who is away has been filled. They expect the eighteen year old to switch roles immediately and become a different kind of member. They do not understand the need this young person has for the church. Jill has seen this happen with her friends' older brothers and sisters and wants it to be different with her. She hopes the church will be as important to her in the next few years as it has been during the past decade.

More than anything else she desires to keep in touch with the significant others in the church who have been her role models. The most important of these is the youth group leader who met with her to discuss career options. This leader must understand that Jill still needs her. Her visible interest and contact through letters and telephone are ways the church has to give Jill a sense of continuity and stability in an otherwise unstable time of her life. During her time of questioning and testing, Jill needs a significant other, an adult with whom she can discuss options, problems, and opportunities. The church has provided such a person at other times in her life, and Jill sees no reason for not expecting the church to keep in contact with her through a person.

It takes time and effort on the part of the congregation to extend its ministry to Jill now that she is away from the community. During the past decade Jill has been an important part of the youth group. She has contributed her time and energy to several programs in the church. Even though conflicts with work and school activities during her last year in high school prevented her from being a regular attender at youth group, she attended worship regularly. She considers the church to be an important force in her life. Of particular importance is the counsel and caring listening of the youth leader.

The church's role does not include making decisions or choices for Jill. It does include giving Jill encouragement to maintain Christian values. These have been instilled in Jill's life through church school teachers, experiences at retreats, and youth group learnings. In many ways, these values have been absorbed without too much questioning. Now she is away from home in quite a different setting and must bring many of these teachings up for review. She needs to see how they can be applied in her new surroundings. She needs to feel that her growth in understanding Christian life values did not stop when she graduated from high school. She needs the continual input and opportunity for dialogue that Christian values require.

The church back home can provide some of this continuing growth. It can keep in touch by mailing books, sermons, bulletins, and devotional materials. It can help Jill find a church away from home by contacting pastors in her new community to introduce her. Of crucial importance is the congregation's recognition that its ministry with and to Jill has not ceased.

The ministry to an eighteen year old who is away at school is different from what it was when she was at home. Now the church must work with a young adult whose decisions will shape the future. In Jill's case, if she pursues biogenetics, her career could drastically revise theological dialogue about humanity's role and responsibility in the creative process. The church must continue to influence her values.

Keeping in touch with Jill is necessary and difficult at this time. She may be distracted from responding to the church's contacts by the demands of her schedule and her need to test her values and life ways. This does not relieve the church of its opportunity to keep before her the Christian basis of a life pattern. This opportunity comes as she talks with her significant others by phone, as she visits her home church, as the church makes certain that she receives materials regularly, and as her pastor keeps in touch with her. The church's interchange with Jill may be awkward at times, but this reflects her insecurity at dealing with adults more than anything else. It does not mean that she resents or resists the continued contact.

Jill is one of the students who chooses not to participate in the campus ministry program at college. She prefers the intergenerational mix of a regular congregation. She can't motivate herself to join one but visits two different churches from time to time. She wants her home church to continue to be her religious contact while she is in college.

The home church must understand how important its relationship is to Jill. In 1995 she is beginning preparation for a career. She has made a decision with implications that are shaping her future. The next few years will be a time of testing and experimenting. The church's role is to be there with her. It does this by insisting that significant others from the church keep in touch with her, by making certain that Jill regularly receives materials for learning and devotion and that she is introduced and guided into a relationship with a church where she now resides. If the church fulfills those roles well, Jill will be more ready to assume new responsibilities when she graduates from college and begins her career in the year 2000.

FIVE

Getting Started in 2000

After graduating from college, Jill decided to complete a one-year, advanced degree program to give herself more competence in biology. New discoveries and experiments in biology continue to occur, and she wanted to spend an extra year learning some of the techniques of genetics that will change human life in the new century. Much of her time is spent in the library at a computer terminal. She is able to read about and to do research on most of what is happening around the world by using the computer. Her study time this year is much more productive than it was during college because she is focused in her interest and because the library computer has finally become part of a world library system. This doesn't mean that everything is available here, but the bibliography of references in her field includes the contributions of important scholars and researchers from every country.

She is being taught, during this year, to perfect her presentations of material via television. She wants to teach in a less urbanized area of the nation and knows she must use television. Typically in these school districts, class sessions are conducted by means of two-way television monitors. She might be the biology teacher for three high schools in a county. This means that the number of students she will instruct can be as high as eight hundred, most of whom will never see her in person. Being able to work as a teacher in a media-dependent educational system is quite important to her.

Another interest this year has been the course offered by her church on the ethics of a new age. She participated in the class by teaching a unit on biogenetics and ethics. It opened a new vista for her. She had intended to bring her Christian values to bear on her field of study but had not dreamed that the church would provide her an opportunity to share her knowledge.

Indeed, during the past few years she has noticed that the church's program for adults has improved considerably. Several courses a year are offered that help people to express their Christian values in the work place. Many people a few years older than she have been attending. She and they feel a need to learn from each other how the Christian life pattern can be made viable in today's world.

The kinds of jobs she is being offered are as innovative as are the techniques she will use in teaching. She decides that she wants to combine teaching high school with part-time work in a research laboratory. She asked for this combination, thinking that it would be available only for college teachers. However, she discovers that during the past five years such combinations have become more common in high schools. Educators, especially in her field, believe that her work in a lab will keep her abreast of many new discoveries coming each year. She is excited about coupling work and teaching because she can use her experiences as well as textbook examples in her teaching.

One of the more important new discoveries is the ability to control the body's immune response mechanism. This breakthrough has alleviated some of the rejection problems people have had with transplanted organs. Understanding other applications of this discovery will be important for her students.

Another of her concerns is the worldwide antipollution campaign. She has been working on a research project that has examined the long-term effects on life forms of various kinds of pollution. She is convinced that the current campaign to eliminate pollution caused by chemicals, wastes, and energy use must succeed. It has taken several years of false starts before the world community has taken seriously the need to cooperate in eliminating pollutants of the air, water, and earth. She feels a need to include this aspect of biology in her teaching of future generations.

She has been encouraged this past year by the Roman Catholic Church's approval of all forms of birth control. This will help her students have a greater control over their bodies. Of course, many Catholic females have ignored the church's edicts over the years, but this has been hard on them as they have tried to be faithful. Now Jill can teach various forms of birth control without feeling guilty. She knows from some of her Catholic friends' comments how welcome this ruling is.

The commerce department's most recent news release on ocean fish is also of interest to Jill. The decade of training and education in the management of ocean resources, especially fish, has begun to show results. The latest report shows an increase of 50 percent in both the fish population and amount of harvest from the ocean during the past year. This will affect the nutritional level of people in many nations. Her teaching will include information about fish as food and as a cultivatable resource.

She will discuss the effects of the change from chemical-intensive to natural farming methods. She will present the cycle of natural farming, replaced by chemical-intensive agriculture, replaced by natural farming which took place in half a century or within the lifetime of her parents. In discussing this cycle in a nonurban area that understands and uses farming as a source of income, Jill can show the disruptions and costs caused by introducing chemicals into a natural biological system.

The most impressive pieces of information that she will present will be statistics and consequences of the increase in longevity of people. During her lifetime, five years have been added to her life expectancy. With the improvements in health and preventive medicine produced by research in genetic structures, the life expectancy of her students may increase an additional five or more years. This is especially exciting to Jill even though the complications of longer life have become somewhat of a social problem.

She will discuss the effect on livestock production of the artificial wombs now used in animal husbandry. These wombs are designed to carry an animal from conception to birth. While the womb is relatively new, improvements in breeding and genetic structure have been around for several decades now. There is some promise that these procedures will be used in humans if the ethical issues can be resolved.

Changes in the way teaching is done as well as shifts in the approach to biology as a subject have come as she was in college and graduate school. She is excited about them and looks forward to trying her skills in real-life situations. She hasn't participated, except as an interested bystander, in the debates that have accompanied these discoveries and policy shifts.

Not only has she gained and used new skills during her year of graduate study, but she has continued to test her values and Christian concepts of life. These tests began when she moved away from home. Since then she has had to evaluate her ideas and actions and then revise and incorporate them into her life pattern. She has begun to realize that putting blame for decisions on others doesn't relieve her of responsibility to choose between alternatives. For instance, while in college she found when she didn't pay her bills on time that she was punished. She discovered that being late or skipping class was a loss to her more than to anyone else. She began to see that her effort in class had a direct bearing on her grades.

These were not unexpected learnings, but they became more important because she saw them bearing directly on her actions. She had to accept responsibility for the consequences of what she did. This was painful during the first two years of college, but by the third and certainly into the fourth year she had willingly assumed her actions as her responsibilities. She came to acknowledge that her values had to be reflected by what she did. She determined how her life was being lived no matter how much she hoped that conversations with peers, parents, and significant others would relieve her of decision making.

Sometime during her second year at college, she realized that biogenetic research was not what she wanted to do full time for a lifetime. She had to agree with her high school counselor: her interest was in people. She didn't feel like being cooped up in a laboratory. She was an active person and working as though caged wasn't a good way for her to live. Thus she had changed her career objective.

She focused her energies during the last two years of college to become a biology teacher. She thought that, in this field, she could combine her interests and her aptitudes. In making this change in life goals, she had acted more independently than ever before. She had looked inward and evaluated her life carefully for the first time with little assistance from other people. After a time of thinking about this shift, she made the change and felt good about herself.

A person thinks of life's turning points as events like getting out of school, taking a job, getting married, receiving a promotion, and having a family. For most of us, any one of these is an event that shapes our future. The added responsibilities that such changes bring make a difference in our lives. But the small daily choices that accumulate over time form the structure on which a life pattern is built. For example, a person is not dramatically changed the day after being married. It takes years of learning to express love in many small ways before one comes to a mature understanding of marriage.

None of the experiences of life are lost even though a person of Jill's twenty-three years will feel most of what she has been doing is a prelude to the best which is yet to come. Her Christian values have taught her to be future oriented. She knows that the sins, forgiveness, and loves of today are the basis for new ventures in discipleship tomorrow. She, like us, keeps the contradictions, insecurities, and disappointments locked in memory. She takes them out occasionally to renew her commitment and to recognize God's grace in her life. As the years extend into the future, she increasingly will accept responsibility for her actions and plans. Those plans and responsibilities evidence her willingness to work with God.

Jill's acceptance of her share of responsibility in working through God in the creative process becomes more pronounced when she moves from college into the work force. She is leaving the easily defined world of a student with its special demands and privileges. She will be required to set up a different kind of structure for her life. The keystone to this new existence is her job, which consumes a third of each day. She wants to use the remainder of the hours of the day in a constructive manner.

The misuse of time is sinful according to her understanding of Christian stewardship.

As she moves from her preparation into the work place, she will find that the Christian values she has nurtured, tested, and accepted as the basis for her life pattern will need to be expressed through words and action. While she may feel good about herself and her background, she will find that she must live in the present, which is constantly changing. The present, 2000 A.D., brings several challenges to her. The manner in which she meets them will determine how well she has built her Christian base.

Choosing a Career and a Family Style

Jill chose a career when she decided to take a job as a teacher and a researcher. Her choice was made in a school environment. As she begins working, she will affirm, modify, or reject her selection. How she adjusts her goals and expectations will depend partly on peer acceptance of her and her efforts and partly on her continuing interest in a career she thought would be rewarding and useful. Her choice was final, she thought, but as she associates with peers beyond the limiting atmosphere of college, she will discover that a career decision is not as binding as she had figured it to be.

Her new peers at the laboratory include women who work part time like she does except that they are combining a career and a family. Most of the people in the laboratory are married, a few for the second time. Among her teacher friends are several with advanced degrees who combine work and teaching as she does. Two have businesses at home that are computer dependent. These enterprises generally are leading training workshops or doing research. Most of the teachers are married, and only two of the twenty on the faculty have been divorced.

Something she expected but which still surprised her was the range of ages of the people with whom she works. She found women and men who are the same age and even older than her parents. At first she was intimidated because she was not accustomed to having older persons as peers. Until now her associates were her age, and those older than she had been authority figures. As she starts work, she must adjust her self-image to accept the fact that she is an adult. No longer is she a student. Her peers have different life goals and different kinds of responsibilities than her student peer group. This colors the lunch table conversation, determining the kinds of experiences that are discussed.

Jill is single and finds that working in a world populated by married persons makes life a bit lonely. It's not that there are so few singles around. Conversely, a large number of single people of her age and older live in the community. However, the difficulty for Jill is that almost all the people she works with are married. This makes her feel somewhat conspicuous. Nevertheless, these are her peers, and she must make friends from among them. She is somewhat surprised that her choice of friends comes primarily from among other faculty members rather than people in the work group. The life goals she holds are more in keeping with her faculty friends than with genetic researchers.

Her choice of other faculty members as her primary peer group will reenforce her decision to teach as a career. Their lunch table conversation and shared experiences will acculturize Jill into an education mold. Her interests will be related to her teaching. This doesn't mean that the laboratory will have no influence. Its impact will be to advance her knowledge and, in some cases, to be a negative support for her values. This latter occurs when the researchers display no feelings for the possible damage a new form of gene mutation may have on an unborn baby. She can't divorce her Christian values from her work even though others in the laboratory seem able to do so.

No one has talked to her specifically about a life or family style. Jill is surprised to discover that she is considered to be a single-person family. Her idea of family has been the kind in which she grew up. She never thought of herself as being a family. But the government says that she is and counts her as a one-person family. She is one of many million single persons living alone or with nonrelatives at the turn of the century.

She has a small apartment, room would be a more apt description, in a house close to her school. The older woman who rents her the room has had several people live with her over the years. She gives Jill total freedom to come and go and allows her to use the kitchen as she desires. Once in a while Jill eats with the woman, but generally each of them prefers to eat alone. Jill's room is next to a bathroom that she doesn't share with anyone else. Jill enjoys being independent and having privacy for the first time since she moved away from home to go to college.

Her greatest expense, she discovers, is for use of the telephone. She insisted on putting in a separate line because she knew she would attach her computer to it. She uses the computer to continue her research as well as to get updates from the laboratory on days she doesn't work there. She keeps a library card (key word) at the university three hundred miles away and accesses it by computer. This has been very helpful during the first few months of work because she has had to reread several text books as she revised her course outlines. She can go to the local library if she needs to have a page or illustration reproduced from a book she reads by computer hookup.

The telephone is important also to keep in touch with her close friends and her family. It is her link to the past and a tool to use as she tests new decisions with people who understand and appreciate her. She sometimes uses the picture part of the phone but prefers to turn it off most of the time when she talks. On special occasions like birthdays or anniversaries she uses the picture to enhance the conversation.

Her automobile is small but is not a commuting car. It is large enough to use on long trips. She had considered buying one of the smaller commuting autos but decided that it didn't have the versatility she needed. She saves the car for out-of-town trips and uses public transportation for most local trips. However, the buses don't run after eight o'clock at night; so if she wishes to go out, she must drive or go by taxi. Even though she is committed to conserving energy, she drives rather than take a cab.

After a month or two of looking around, she found a church. She isn't interested in most other kinds of organizations although she is a nominal member of the environmental impact committee. She was put on this town committee because of her teaching position at the high school. She has not joined any specific group within the church yet, preferring instead to attend worship and to become acquainted. She is encouraged to stay by the number of people her age in attendance and likes the educational program for adults in which she participates often.

Her choices of life pattern and career are in keeping with her long-term Christian values. She lives simply and deals with her career as an expression of her commitment. She doesn't articulate this very well; in fact, she hasn't talked publicly about her career as a ministry. She probably won't in the near future. She doesn't talk easily about those things. Instead she tries to live according to the values she has accepted as her own. She feels these are Christian but continues to test her actions against what the church teaches.

She isn't as certain of her choices in private as she appears to be in public. She is uncertain and insecure but discovers that other people her age and older have the same kind of questioning. That is the reason going to church is so helpful to her. Not only the minister but members of the adult classes also share their insights as well as faith.

She discovers an interesting young man at church. He is not a teacher but is in business for himself. He works as a freelance computer programmer. Much of his work is done at his computer in his home. He might, on the other hand, be called to any part of the nation to spend a week working out a problem for a company. Jill has begun to have special feelings for him but has misgivings as well. She finds herself moving toward another major decision point in her life.

Whether or Not to be Married

Both Jill's mother and father worked outside the home. She has seen her family combine two careers with a minimum of conflict; her father had taken at least half of the responsibility for the household. These images of family life are the basis for her consideration of marriage. The main question is "Do I want to get married?" Her mother would not have had to face such a question, but that was years ago. Now an unmarried career woman has as much status as a woman with a family or as a man.

The decision to get serious with a man implies that Jill may need to contemplate marriage. She must consider whether she wants to continue as a single career person, a working wife, or a nonworking wife. While the final choice among these options may wait a while, the need to make a selection has to be acknowledged.

As she considers her choice, she will talk over her options with several persons. Her current peer group among the faculty may not be appropriate. She might not know the members well enough or trust them to know her long-range intentions. Thus, she contacts two of her close friends from college days. One of them has married, and the other is pursuing a career in business. Her conversations with them alert her to the advantages of increased income, the problems with schedules, the difficulties in deciding to have children, and the opportunities for travel. She can't make a final determination based on their suggestions.

She turns to her adult friends in her home church. She has maintained a good relationship with them over the years and has listened to their advice. One of them encouraged her to try her hand at teaching, for example. She explains her dilemma, and she and her adult friends discuss it over the phone. In three days she receives a letter as well. The gist of both the telephone conversation and the letter is that the decision must be based on the kind of person she selects for a mate. This individual must have certain characteristics, the most promi-nent of which are compatible values, the willingness to support and help her as a career person, and attitudes similar to hers regarding how a marriage is entered into and maintained.

Her next tactic is to ask her parents to come for a visit. During the two days they spend with her, she discusses her future and tries to clarify her thinking about a mate. They share their experiences and register their cautions but add that the decision is hers to make. They meet the man who is interested in Jill. They comment on their impressions of him but are careful to be supportive of her. They do not make her choice.

The process she uses in making this decision is similar to the one she uses when she makes any choice. She considers her own interests and goals; she tests the idea with close friends; she tentatively decides; and then she seeks approval from her support base, in this instance, her parents. During this entire time she is questioning, talking about, and testing the idea with the man and in informal sessions with associates at work and on the faculty. Her decisions are made in a social context. Therefore, she must ask others to help her by giving their suggestions.

She knows, at twenty-three, that her final decision will be her own responsibility. She is aware that such a choice will carry with it other choices; perhaps the most important one is where she will live.

A Place to Live

Jill decided, as she chose her job, to live in a nonurban surrounding. She had grown up in a suburb and wanted some relief from the rapid pace of urban life. She was reflecting the attitude of many young people in the late 1990s who opted for life beyond the city. She and they felt that the computer connection they had with the world was sufficient to keep them abreast of happenings in their field. Television would keep them informed about happenings in the world. In addition, they traveled to large urban centers at least semiannually for conferences and seminars for career-related updates. Her selection of a place to live and a job made sense to Jill when she completed her year of graduate study.

She expected her first job to last between two and five years. She wanted a testing time at the start of her career in which to learn and to determine how well she liked teaching and research work. She had no intention of remaining in a nonurban setting her entire life.

Another factor in setting her time limit was her conviction that a nonurban environment had too few opportunities for her children to participate in cultural activities and events if she should decide to get married and to have a family. Her intent was not to consider marriage for at least another six or seven years. Suddenly, in her first year as a career person, she is confronted with an opportunity to become serious with a young man.

Her most immediate choice is whether to move in with him or to remain in her apartment. While many couples her age live together to reduce living costs, she doesn't feel that such an arrangement allows her the freedom to make up her mind about marriage and especially marriage to this person. She discovers that the young man holds the same view. She also knows that this community is his hometown. He grew up here and wants to remain near his family.

Her experiment with nonurban living has been carefully planned and of limited duration. When she contemplates marriage, she has to rethink that decision from the perspective of her long-term career plans and the location consequences of marrying this particular man. She understands his desire to live close to his family. She has been separated by several hundred miles from her parents during college and has kept in touch by telephone and infrequent visits. She feels it might be a good idea for her to live closer to them. Given his preference for living in the community, her desire to live closer to her parents might cause tension in a new marriage.

However, since he prefers to remain in this place, she begins to look more closely at the community as she works in her school and at her laboratory. She must evaluate the benefits and disadvantages of living in this setting for several years. She has to think about career advancement. Can she get the recognition she needs by working and living here?

As she thinks about it, place doesn't seem to matter as much now as it has for previous generations. The current computer networks available to most households make intellectual, monetary, and consumer exchange easy. She would not be hindered by living here so long as she attends the semi-annual professional meetings. In fact, her arrangement of teaching and research might be very difficult to match in a more urban setting.

Her big problem here is at school. She has to produce television class sessions each day. She isn't accustomed to being on stage as a teacher. On the other hand she knows that without using television as a teaching tool, students in outlying communities would not have a chance to take a biology course. Perhaps, if she stayed, she could use a different school as home base each year. That way she could get to know the students as people rather than as images asking questions on a television monitor.

. Another factor affecting her choice is whether she wants to continue as a public school teacher or teach in the private high school in the county. Budget problems in public school systems have hindered them for the past two decades. In addition, the quality of education they provide has been seriously questioned. Many people, especially more affluent professional families, have helped to create and sustain innovative private schools. These place emphasis on low teacher-to-student ratios, use of electronic technology for teaching and research, and high standards of continuing education for faculty. In many ways these alternative private schools are elitist, and this bothers Jill.

Yet the pay is better and the facilities are more modern in the private school. Research facilities for students are better and the use of computers and television to reach private feeder schools are more sophisticated. If she opts for the private system, she will need to move to another community that is about half an hour away. As she considers this option, she discovers that her values push her toward the public rather than the private system. As she analyzes her feelings, she decides that the key factor in her choice revolves around providing the best education possible for those who are on the lower echelons of economic opportunity. Among them are many students who have immigrated to this area and have difficulty with language. She decides that her proficiency in Spanish can be used best in the public rather than in the private school system.

Still another important consideration in choosing where to live is the cultural opportunities available here as opposed to those of an urban setting. Television with its satellite transmissions can bring the world into her room, but she misses the liveliness of stage productions. When she was growing up, her family went into the city to see plays, concerts, and even a ballet. She enjoyed those excursions and knows the quality of local productions will never approach the caliber of professional performances in the city.

Living in a nonurban area doesn't mean isolation. She can travel to a city easily and quickly by plane or train. If she wants, she can go abroad. She can be in London in three hours if she wants to see productions there. The speed and ease of travel alleviate her fear of not having cultural experiences for herself and her potential family.

Her primary limitation for travel is its cost. So long as she is careful about money, she can take at least one long trip a year. If she had the freedom of schedule like her parents who work part time, she could take advantage of the lower off season rates. But she can't and must plan better.

She recognizes that the total atmosphere of this community will influence her thinking and way of living. She believes that the moral attitudes of the community must coincide with her value system or she will feel uncomfortable and be an outsider as long as she resides here. Not only are the churches and their influence important but equally influential is the morality expressed through the schools and businesses in the community. She can abide the slower pace of life so long as the underlying values of the town undergird her own. It will take a year or two of testing and exploring before she can make that determination.

Meanwhile she has found herself comparing where she is and what she does with where her parents are and how they deal with life. She finds herself reestablishing contact with them as an adult peer rather than as a daughter.

Finding Personal Roots

The artificial environment of college has been replaced by a demanding world of change for Jill. Her choices and decisions have no precedent in her life. She is creating experiences against which future options will be measured. For the first time in her life she is on her own. The peer groups she establishes at her work places are more competitive and less supportive than any she has had in the past. She discovers that no longer is she a girl who is preparing for a career but a woman with a career.

Readjusting her social image is relatively easy because she continues to act, dress, and work with the intensity she has brought to every task in the past and with the charm she acquired during the past decade. She has learned how to function effectively in social situations because of the teachings of peer groups during high school and college. Her dress and general behavior are results of learnings gotten after she left home.

Underlying this social image is her personal concept of what she is. This has been evolving for as long as she can remember. The most important contributors to this image have been her parents. They gave her, through their attention, criticisms, and love, a feeling about herself and toward the world in which she lives. Even though she rejected their life pattern when she left home to attend college, she finds that she cannot divorce herself from its major tenets once she is in the working world. In particular, she finds herself wanting to get their opinion about potential life-changing decisions before making final ones.

The family's roots are crucial to the twenty-three year old who is attempting to be a productive individual for the first time in her life. She is alone except for those memories and values that have stood the test of her years. Keeping in touch with those who gave her the roots becomes quite important during these first months on her own. The insecurity of making all her decisions by herself must be offset by reestablishing ties with the family. This doesn't mean that she will let her parents make her decisions. What she needs most is to feel that they are available to her and can be counted on in her time of need. She depends on them to help her think through major decisions that she faces.

Their role is not to be protectors but to be listeners and suggesters. They should not believe that Jill needs them in the same way she needed them in the past. She is an adult and has assumed responsibility for her own life. Now she desires a base that she can touch when she feels alone. She has to trust a person or persons whose experiences can somehow parallel her own. She has peer groups, but they aren't the "safe" or supportive kind she had before. She hasn't decided to marry yet and doesn't have a mate to talk with about life-shaping events. She returns to her parents and will keep this tie viable during the remainder of their life if they can accept her as an adult.

Jill is discovering that she must have a base to return to periodically. She must have people to talk with who understand how to cope effectively with pressures of work, community, and peers. Helping her cope is the primary function of her parents at this point.

Coping

Each individual must learn coping skills. People learn to cope by mimicking or adapting other peoples' behavior in similar situations. Jill has been fortunate to have lived in a dormitory because coping skills were worked out there in a supportive atmosphere. High school also was as much a time to learn social coping skills as it was a time to add knowledge. School, in fact, is a social laboratory in which getting along with others is as much a part of the education as are the courses.

Jill soon finds that every group to which she relates places a set of pressures on her. Each group's expectations and rules of behavior are different because they are related to the interests of that particular group and place. For instance, the pressures of her bosses and colleagues have little to do with her private life but say much about her use of time, development of skill, and ability to work well with others. These pressures are result oriented and are intense most of the time.

Pressures from peers relate mostly to the intersecting of their private lives. In this arena Jill's values and attitudes are tested. Her willingness to reveal her values in lunchroom discussions or during informal breaks is an indication of her feeling that her beliefs are compatible with those of her peers. If she feels she is out of line with the majority of her peers, it is likely that she will keep quiet. In time she may decide that she doesn't want to associate with them at all and will seek another job.

The interaction with the man in whom she is interested produces another kind of pressure. Their dates and her feelings emphasize unresolved decisions regarding her future. The longer that she continues their relationship, the more intense becomes the pressure to choose. Even if she entered into the relationship only because of a need for companionship, over time the liaison creates pressures on her future.

Reestablishing ties with her parents carries additional pressures. Jill knows that they have expectations of her and opinions about appropriate behavior. While they are careful not to comment on her life pattern, she knows how they feel about most everything she does. At least she thinks she knows how they feel, and she feels internal pressure when she doesn't act as she thinks they want her to behave. Most of the time she doesn't share with them actions that she feels might upset them or indicate how much she has changed.

Finally, Jill must cope with the pressures of community expectations. These relate to the social image of a single, female teacher in the public high school. As much as she would like to be her own person, she finds that in the community's eyes she has a social image, which was created by others and to which she must somehow adapt or change. This pressure is exerted on her by school administrators, townspeople, and students. It seems to be never ending and is so subtle that she finds it difficult to describe.

She learns how to cope with these pressures by talking with two of her close friends from college, her peers at work, other adults at church, and her parents. Each of these social groups provides insight and assistance to Jill. She discovers that others have the same pressures she feels and they need her assistance in meeting them. Jill has taken another step. She learns that she is a constructive member of several groups. That learning gives her a new feeling of importance and worth.

In her process of growth during the year, she has depended upon the church quite a lot. She doesn't understand how her friends and associates can ignore it so easily. It has meant much to her even though she can't put her finger on exactly what it has done.

The Church's Role

Jill is fortunate to attend a church that performs four roles essential to her Christian growth. It has an education program for adults that tackles issues of interest and concern to her. It accepts her as an adult: when she declines invitations to participate in groups or to lead, it accepts the refusal with an affirmation that she will be approached at another time after she has become more acclimated to the community. It offers her fellowship among people of her age group who are single or married. It confirms her feeling—that she is an individual worth knowing and having as part of the congregation—by visiting her on the phone and in person.

She knows some people her age are put off by church contacts. But the woman who seems to have made her a personal mission appears interested in her and her work. She checks on Jill when she doesn't attend worship and invites her to various social activities she thinks Jill might enjoy. She hasn't pushed herself on Jill but has let her know that she wants to be a friend.

When a congregation performs these roles well for a twenty-three year old, it is not surprising that she will feel positive toward the church and yet not be able to point specifically at a reason. Its willingness to let her be involved as she desires is its primary characteristic. However, if it didn't have an adult education program dealing with issues of interest to her, she might not find it very attractive. It is hard for an outsider to break into established adult programs unless she has a sponsor. It is easier to get involved when classes are not fixed in membership. Jill happened to pick such a congregation.

She finds the people in the church, at class and during fellowship times, willing to discuss faith and theology with her. She hasn't spoken about her faith for some time (it wasn't a popular topic in the dormitory), and she feels good about being able to get other viewpoints on ethics and faith. She finds the give and take helpful in reaffirming as well as adjusting some of her ideas. The adult atmosphere of these sessions helps her to move from adolescent thought patterns she still depends on in her faith. It is during one of these class discussions that she begins to think of her job as a form of personal ministry. This is a new and powerful way of looking at her career.

Any shift in regarding her job as a ministry rather than as a career has an important consequence. She will not find it easy to quit teaching. If it is a ministry, it becomes a lifelong task. However, her new friends caution her not to lock herself into a particular type of teaching. Instructing people can be done in many ways and in several different settings.

Perhaps her greatest pleasure at the church is being treated as an adult person. She is expected to contribute to the groups and services she attends. She is not allowed to hide but is actively sought out as a potential leader. Even though she resists the invitations, she is happy that others see her potential. Of particular importance to her are the minister's visits. Not only did she visit immediately after Jill first came to the church, but she has been back two additional times during the few months Jill has been attending. These visits from the pastor make Jill feel wanted.

This congregation has looked at the needs of people at various stages in life. It has consciously chosen to meet those needs by special programs. The congregation is not large, but its members are concerned. They have made it their ministry to help each other as a community of faith. Jill has found them and, once again, feels security in her values and life pattern. She will need this base as she matures and takes on other challenges. These will focus for her during the next five years.

SIX

Focusing Her Life
in 2005

The eight-year-old child we met in the mid-1980s is twenty-eight this year. Her world is adult. She has learned to view herself as an independent person with skills and worth. Her value system is in place and is supported by her peer groups at work and at church. This base is quite important because she will be required to make life-changing decisions within the next few months. Tranquility in her world is not a long-term companion.

She currently holds jobs that she had five years ago. Therefore, she continues to live and work in the nonurban setting we learned about then. She was married last fall to the young man she met at church. Their plans are to live in their present community for no more than a year. After that they hope to find a position for Jill in a city close to Jill's parents' home.

Her husband is a telecommunications expert and works for a national consulting network. It makes no difference where he lives because he regularly keeps in touch with his home office by computer. Most of his travel is to clients; he checks into his office by phone only once a month. He is in control of his schedule much of the time.

The young family lives in one of the new apartment complexes in their community. They considered purchasing a home, but it was too costly both in the monthly payments and the required down payment. They decided to invest part of their monthly income in lieu of strapping themselves with a heavy mortgage commitment. They made this decision in spite of pressures from family and friends to buy a home. They wanted freedom to move within a short time and knew that investing in a home would make this impossible.

The apartment complex in which they live houses young couples like themselves as well as many of the single persons who constitute about a third of the community's population. The residents chose this life pattern because of the high cost of other types of housing.

Jill and her husband consider this living arrangement temporary, but they like the conveniences of apartment living. As a result, they are contemplating purchasing one of the row houses common in recent housing developments in cities. They don't feel a need, right now, to buy a single family house in a suburb as their parents did years ago.

Jill's life is unsettled just now. She had begun to feel comfortable with her jobs and her living style. After deciding to get married, she had to confront decisions about where to live and whether to continue her career; she had to adjust her life pattern once again. She had thought through some implications of such choices previously, and that made her decisions somewhat easier. Nevertheless, picking the correct alternative was not assured and the process generated insecurity for her. Even though she talks about her potential direction with others, the instability of new situations still bothers her.

One other problem has surfaced since marriage. Jill and her husband haven't decided finally whether to have a family. They have put this off for a year or two, but Jill knows the ultimate choice is hers. She has ambivalent feelings about it even though her mother's role model illustrated that combining a career and a family is possible. Jill isn't certain that she wants to live with the stress of a career while caring for a child. Her generation has been taught that building a solid home life for a family is as important as succeeding in a career. She needs time to consider her long-range intentions.

Her eventual choice about a family will affect where the family settle. The choice of living in the city included the stipulation that she and her husband evaluate their experience in a year. If they don't like city living, they are committed to making different arrangements probably by purchasing a home in a suburb. Her husband's background in a small town and hers in a suburb seem to point to their eventual location in a single family house in a suburb or nonurban area. Their tentative choice is a suburb because it holds a better possibility for Jill to continue her career. Meanwhile they intend to take advantage of the city's public transportation system and use their one auto for travel outside the city.

They expect to continue to live simply, which is another reason for choosing to live in an apartment at first. They wanted to build up some financial reserves and take their time in picking out a place to live which is suited to their simple life pattern.

Their attitudes reflect their basic value systems. They grew up when conservatism was stressed as a necessity in a Christian life pattern. The societal mood, which initiated recycling and environmental protection more than three decades ago, has produced a society of young people who are accustomed to saving and reusing materials.

A result of this conserving emphasis is clothing apparel made almost entirely of natural fibers such as cotton and wool. Almost no clothing is made of synthetic fibers. Cotton and similar commodities have been improved considerably by hybrid seeds mutated during the past two decades. Wool has increased in popularity especially among those who have been battling frigid winters that plague the nation every five years or so.

Jill's diet doesn't include coffee or tea. These drinks are no longer popular. The long-term trend away from their use, begun more than two decades ago, has resulted in near elimination of them from most households. They were victims of the health consciousness on which Jill was raised. Her carefully monitored nutritional intake is matched by a stringent exercise program. She considers her body part of God's gift and feels that it deserves her best stewardship.

Jill is pleased with her father's new job. This is the fourth occupation change for him that she can remember. Her mother has changed occupations twice. Now as her parents are in their early sixties, both of them have found less demanding jobs that will allow them to work for at least another decade. They, like many other near retirees before them, do not plan to retire. They expect to work at least part time for the foreseeable future.

Jill has been impressed with the manner in which her parents have handled aging. Of course, society is much more age conscious now than when she was young. Job changes are expected and older folks shift jobs more readily. Part-time work, work with extended leaves, and consultant work have become popular variations in many older persons' work lives. These are reasons behind the number of job changes for both of her parents. They adjusted their work schedule to their age, interest, and energy levels.

Her parents' pensions were funded by each of their former employers. The funded pensions have given them freedom to work at a different pace as their lives have moved through various cycles.

During the past few years, Jill's parents have traveled extensively. They took Jill with them on their most recent trip abroad. She found this a good way to relate to them. She felt quite relaxed after that month.

War threats of the late 1990s have subsided somewhat, but peace doesn't seem possible. A consequence of the many conflicts around the world is the continuing stream of immigrants into the United States every year. While her community receives a few of these displaced families, the urban centers on each coast are the primary entry points for them. The resulting violence and disruptions in these cities make life in those areas unappealing to Jill and many other young people.

A significant change in the world has occurred by the commercial use of nuclear fission as a fuel. The steel industry began using this form of energy the past three years. People close to the new plants are afraid that an accident will cause a catastrophe nearly as great as the one created when the power plant in the Midwest leaked radioactivity in the early 1990s. Jill considered the location of these plants when she and her husband selected a place to live. She wanted at least a hundred miles between her house and such a plant.

She has been pleased with her teaching position primarily because of the reaction of her students. They have been interested in learning. Discipline has not been a problem. Her peers say they have seen students' attitudes change drastically in the past decade. They think it is because of increased stability in family life. This is in marked contrast to the instability Jill saw as she grew up. Not only has the divorce rate decreased dramatically, but as more people work in their homes, stronger families are developed. Few people would have predicted this result from the use of home computers, but it has happened. She is pleased with the prospect of raising her children, if she decides to have any, in a community with a strong family emphasis.

She doesn't think she wants to do it, but she could determine the sex of her child. Sex choice, she believes, ought to remain with the creative process even though many couples select their child's sex. At the same time, she is happy that most of the serious inheritable deformities can be controlled by drugs and gene splicing. She and her husband will have to be tested soon to see if there are possible problems they might correct before a child is conceived.

Her aim continues to be to maintain the Christian values that have sustained and guided her in the past. She has adapted them to adult situations but knows that they must be evaluated regularly by daily experience. Attending church and participating in adult education courses have been two important activities she has used to sustain the imprint of her values in her life. She knows that moving to a city and living in a strange environment will require a change in her religious habits. She wonders how well she can adapt this critical part of her life.

This next year will be a time of testing for Jill and her husband. Some of the decisions they make will create unexpected adventures and problems in later life. No one is able to foresee exactly what the consequences of their choices will be, but we can examine the more immediate results of some selections.

Career? Family? Both?

As an individual Jill has picked from among options for the past decade. She has enjoyed the freedom and responsibility of being able to determine her own life's direction. Shortly after she married, she realized that selecting among alternatives was not her sole prerogative. Choosing became a joint venture with her husband. This caused her some difficulty in their early months. She discovered that he had the same tensions as she in making decisions about his life pattern. They agreed that they must discuss any choice they confronted in their careers before they made it. Marriage meant working together. Both of them were committed to strengthening their relationship and making their marriage a stable base from which they journeyed into the world.

Therefore the choice of continuing her career was a topic of serious conversation. Her husband was home at least half of his working time. This made coming home after work nice for her. They could relax together for a while before having to fix a meal or prepare for an evening meeting. When he was gone, Jill reverted to habits acquired during her decade of being single. This pattern of life was comfortable to both of them.

As they considered moving, Jill broached the possibility of quitting one of her jobs and being a part-time worker. They didn't need the money from her two incomes, and she felt that their free time might be used for travel, additional education, or leisure. It might be advisable for her husband to adjust his work schedule to part time as well.

This line of reasoning pointed out to both of them that their life pattern was simpler and less complicated than others around them. Yet the choice they faced had been made many times by other couples who were trained and were in the job force. The primary goal for each of them was personal development, which included creating a strong family life.

Jill was considering combining a career and marriage much like 60 percent of the women in the nation. It seemed natural, and businesses made it much more convenient to adjust schedules than they had in the past, according to her mother's stories. Not only could she combine a career and a marriage, she could have a job and a family as well. But she had not made her final decision yet. The couple's desires at present were to move into the city and to let Jill have a part-time job. Making the job decision was a hard choice because she had to pick between teaching and working as a researcher.

When the move came, however, the decision between teaching and research had to be remade because the city they selected offered Jill the opportunity to pursue both careers. The decision to work part time in one field had to be reviewed by both of them. Their revised choice was for Jill to work full time by combining her two careers, just as she had done since graduate school. This affected their plans for travel and leisure and postponed her goal of studying for another advanced degree. It was a difficult choice for them to make, and it created tensions in their relationship.

Jill felt relieved after they agreed that her combined career should last no more than three or four years. She didn't see any need to hold two jobs when she and her husband didn't require the income. Besides, she wanted to work less and spend more time with her husband.

Her greatest difficulty at her next career decision point will be to choose between being a teacher or being a researcher. Both fascinate her. At the same time, while having a career is fine, her goals are becoming more intertwined with those of her husband: they want to strengthen their relationship. Career advancement, no matter what her selection of field, is becoming secondary. She and he are like many other young people their age in 2005 who are deciding to live frugally and concentrate on maintaining and strengthening their family life.

As she thinks about their revised decision, she is forced to admit that it isn't a long-term solution. She begins to feel that her choices must fit life situations she and her husband create rather than being a replica of someone else's life pattern. The pattern of their life is being developed; they aren't copying anyone else. What she is trying to do is to keep the Christian values she has depended on, concepts of personal ministry and stewardship, in the forefront as she selects options. She seeks, through her work and relationships, to exemplify love, forgiveness, and commitment. These are the cornerstones on which her life and family, now, are based. She wishes, wistfully, for a world in which decisions once made would last for a long time. However, the only choice she sees stretching far into the future is her selection of a mate. She will build her life with his.

The Family Unit

Her entry into marriage was not a swift step. She had known her husband for four years and had dated him for three. They had talked over life goals, careers, and the possibility of children many times. During the year in which they became engaged they felt a growing attraction for each other which extended far beyond physical desire. They were comfortable in each other's presence and agreed generally on ultimate goals. They did not agree on everything and were not inhibited from disagreeing. They handled conflict by bringing it into the open.

After they married, they remained part of their peer groups at work but have noticed a change in the kinds of things they discuss with them. The need to talk about their personal relationships is less pressing than it was before they got married. The conversations with peers now deal with finances, leisure, and job opportunities. Perhaps their lives are changing more than they realize.

The two of them are beginning to depend on each other and a new peer group at church more than they did on former associates. They test their ideas frequently with new rather than old friends. This new peer group is composed mostly of young married couples like themselves. However, it includes a few couples who might be as old as their parents. They found the mix of ages and experience helpful as they struggled with their career and place-to-live decisions. It was this group at church that helped them to list the positives and negatives of the various alternatives. That list was very useful as they finally chose to live in the city and for Jill to continue with both of her careers.

Because the group has been so helpful, Jill dreads the day when she will leave the church. The group members, too, are thinking of the loss but point out that the church lives in other places besides here. They encourage her to look to another congregation and find in it the kinds of assistance she has discovered here. They insist that she not try to use them as a role model because the kinds of choices she and her husband will encounter in their new home will be quite different from those they had to make here. She feels their caution. The main unmade choice for Jill and her husband is whether or not to have children. Jill and her husband had agreed to wait two years before settling this question, but Jill feels, at twenty-eight, that she is at the age when she must make up her mind. After they move into the city and she becomes accustomed to her new jobs, she will have to review her time schedule. She isn't getting younger. Half of the women who give birth have their first child when they are about twenty-seven years old. This statistic has its effect on her.

What changes might a child make in their life? She isn't certain. She is convinced that she will continue with a career, however, she feels she ought to work at only one job. After some soul searching and long discussions with her husband, she decides that that job will be teaching. This isn't an easy choice, but she feels that the students keep her on her toes by their questioning. She likes very much the relationships she has maintained with her classes. In addition, she has gotten used to the television classes and wants to do some special work to send back to her former system. The first choice is to teach part time. That decision will revolutionize her life pattern.

Another basic change of having a family will be to increase the number of people with whom she is intimately related. She will discover that she can feel and display different kinds of love to each of them, husband and child. No longer will she be able to think solely about herself or herself and her husband, but the three of them will become a unit. Health, psychology, and developmental tasks of the child will impinge upon her career. Time for her to be alone will be jeopardized because a child is a constant presence. She has chosen to forgo singleness by getting married. This choice carried with it a different kind of election, whether to have children. When she selects that option, the next decision looms before her—how many children should she have?

Many of her friends from college are engaged in the same kinds of choices. Most of her high school friends who did not go to college have already married, and several have at least two children. A few of her friends, not more than 10 percent, have chosen to remain single and childless. The variety of images she has received from observing these former associates has only a passing influence on her. She has been choosing on the basis of her own values that have been developed along the lines of her parents' and the teachings of the church.

She has not questioned any of her decisions. She has discovered that second guessing is not a productive thing to do. Once she elects a course of action, she lives with its consequences. She is a believer in being free to choose an option and being willing to live with the results, be they expected or unanticipated.

Now that she has made important selections about her family unit, she finds that she and her husband need to revise their life goals. Thinking three instead of two or one makes a significant difference to Jill. Love and commitment take on different qualities in a family setting. Although her goals were established after college, she was beginning to feel their narrowness. Her vision has enlarged, and her responsibilities have increased. More importantly, she has committed herself to a relationship with a particular person and that brings demands she had not considered previously.

Revising Life's Goals

Jill set life goals when she was in high school and followed them into a career. Her decisions to teach in a public school, to work in a biogenetic research laboratory, to go to church, and to consider marriage after five years beyond college were possible because of her goals. If she had not had these stepping stones for life, she would have felt more at loose ends than she did at each decision point. She is satisfied with her choices but knows that it is important to revise and extend her life's intentions. Now she must consider more than herself in making these goals.

She has observed the effects of not having goals in some of her friends' lives. They have been unable to make lasting choices and, in a few instances, have had to reverse decisions. This happened to one of her close friends who is now under a doctor's care. Her friend wanted to get married but couldn't choose between two suitors. She gloried in their attention, but when each of them got serious she got caught in the middle. She became the victim of their jealousy.

Jill has witnessed broken marriages, interrupted careers, and hostile marriage partners because people didn't think about their goals. She doesn't believe that objectives ought to be written in stone, but she feels that living by goals based on values is most productive. She is much more convinced of her position now that she is married. Those goals have led her to this situation. They must be revised so that they can assist her in future decision making.

The choices she has made concerning her career, marriage, and a family have contributed to revising those goals without further contemplation from her. They have nudged her from goals which were single oriented. Her advancement in her career must be balanced by the demands of her family. Already she has elected to pursue one instead of two career paths. This doesn't mean that she will be a teacher for the remainder of her life. It means two other things. First, she will concentrate on one career, and, second, she will reduce her income.

Both of these results from her choice of career goals must reflect her life goals, or her frustration and eventual anger could cause insurmountable difficulties in her life. She must realize that a choice made now determines future options. She found that out when she chose her career. It is reaffirmed as she selects teaching. Her future as a genetic researcher is ended for all practical purposes because she will lose her competency rapidly in this volatile field. She knew this when she made her decision.

Marriage created another opportunity to revise life goals. In their conversations prior to marriage, Jill and her husband tested and revised the parameters of their lives. Their choice of each other was a compromise. Each had an ideal image against which they measured the other. In the long run they selected each other as the best fit for their image. They felt they could live through the differences as they worked out a new image of themselves as a couple.

As they became a family unit, they found that freedom to choose a direction had to become a limited freedom. The limitation related directly to the career and life hopes of each partner. This was a new experience for them both. Yet the more they worked at readjusting their thinking and decision-making processes, the more comfortable they felt with the new checkpoint. They didn't give up freedom so much as they chose to work out decisions jointly. This changed one of the life goals so cherished by them when they were single.

The third decision that impinges on her life goals is that of conceiving a child. The details of living will be worked out as the need occurs, but considering having another person in the family is an important step for Jill. She has found happiness and security in her two-person family. Now, if she goes through with a pregnancy, she will have to establish a new kind of base that includes, for many years, a child for whom she cares. Future choices to have children will not have as much effect on her life goals as the choice to have the first one.

Peer Groups

At this point in her life, peer groups have a limited effect on Jill. Their primary function, as with her church friends, is to test decisions that she has made. This is quite different from the role that former associates have played. In the past, she tested and revised ideas on the basis of their suggestions. Now she tests ideas and gets suggestions from her husband. The family unit is the base from which life-changing choices are now made.

This doesn't mean that peer groups will be unimportant in her future. They will affect the resources she uses, the selection of doctors for her child, the choice of school to which the youngster will be sent, and other similar decisions. None of these will be finalized, however, until the choices have been discussed and approved within the family.

She will change the peer groups to which she relates several times as she lives through child rearing. Each change in the child's age will introduce persons and peers into her life. In fact, as she makes her choice to have a child at age twenty-eight, she will find herself seeking out parents and significant others for advice and counsel. The narrow set of intimate confidants will not be enlarged in later years although those who are her significant others will change from time to time and place to place over the years.

Life Values

Jill's life has become focused on her family and one or two significant others. In large measure this concentration is due to her search for people who can assist her in upholding her life values. She has discovered that everyone is not like her. Even at church she finds few people who adhere to the same set of values as she. Her working companions openly reject one or more of her values. These rejections have helped test her beliefs in another adult forum, but she has lived enough to know that her beliefs are as valid as anyone else's. However, what she needs most is not testing but stable values. The base for her family must be firm. This means that her value system must be in place.

Values change little during a lifetime. Usually they are implanted before a child becomes an adolescent. The outlines of a value system are evident before a child attends school, even though the child is not able to articulate those values. Jill's values were operative when we first met her twenty years ago. She gets in touch with the beliefs that influence her decisions as the need arises. For example, her values about having a child were implanted in early childhood as she experienced her home life and felt the attitudes of her parents toward her. These values were not important, except as she discussed the possibility of children with her peers, until she was faced with actually making a choice about having children.

This doesn't mean that values are unchangeable. Jill's life experiences, especially her career accomplishments, could have affected her desire to have a child. Indeed, she waited until she was twenty-eight to make her choice. In this way her values relative to having a child of her own were revised by her values concerning her adult contribution to a field of endeavor. The revision of values is critical to Jill at age twenty-eight. She must bring to her attention the values that will underlie the decisions she makes the remainder of her life.

Experience will help her deal with her values. She will have to make hard choices between personal impulses and the well-being of her family. She may choose to go with her personal needs, which reflect a part of her value system. This is a factor in her election to proceed with a career even after she has a child. In other situations she may select values that deny some of her personal wants and pick those dealing more with her husband's or child's needs. Jill will not be left alone with a static value system. She will be weighing one set of values against another and making a choice between them continually.

Her husband, child, significant others, and parents are key figures in helping her make decisions about which values to emphasize at any given time. She will find crises easier to deal with than apparently insignificant choices. The latter are much more frequent and accumulate as a life pattern. Crises are confronted by rote decisions based on the life pattern. She must revise those values carefully and remember the importance of "unimportant" choices.

The church plays a significant role in her value and goal revision processes. It is able to accomplish its role successfully only because it has kept in touch with Jill. It has made its programs and people sensitive to age-level needs. Jill has not had the opportunity to withdraw from the church because her congregations have not allowed that to happen. A significant other and a pastor have made it their business through the years to keep Jill related to the church. This hasn't been easy for the church, but there is no other way to make certain that a church plays the proper role in helping a person grow up to be a Christian.

The Church's Role

The church functions in several capacities for Jill. It continues to provide a supportive group in which she can participate. It has an adult education program that has a curricula for every age and condition of adulthood. It helps her to consider her career as a ministry and holds before her ways in which her career relates to the work of the church. It gives, through a neighborhood strategy plan, an opportunity to meet regularly with her neighbors for discussion and spiritual growth. It gives Jill chances to be a leader with any age group she chooses.

A key factor in Jill's life continues to be the fellowship group at church. She has found the members to be supportive and interested. They have listened to her and given their ideas prior to most of her decisions. Her husband came from such a group. She feels at home with them. They have taken the place of her parents during times of illness and depression. This group has been the visible church to her when her skepticism about God and life's purpose have been overshadowed by personal cares.

The supportive fellowship role of the church hasn't come by accident. It has been there because members have been encouraged to be ministers in life. The clergyperson is not the church. Each member is responsible for ministering to other members. It took this congregation several years of effort to create such a feeling and give direction to its life. Because it has this approach, Jill has felt wanted, appreciated, and useful. She is a member because it's exciting to be in ministry.

The longer she has belonged to the church community, the more convinced she is that the supportive and challenging relationships here have guided most of her choices about her life pattern. The attitudes and values in this church have supported her own. This affirmation of her life pattern has made her stronger when the peer groups at work have rejected her values as impractical. She returns to the church group for support in her emphasis upon honesty and integrity.

Another role played by the several congregations of which she has been a member is education. When she was young, she learned values and life patterns. As she went through high school and college, the church's education program evolved to deal with issues she faced then. When she graduated from college and begun a career, she found a congregation with an adult education program that forced her to confront values and life goals. Without these kinds of educational experiences, she would have been a highly skilled and well-trained professional but one whose spiritual growth was juvenile.

She doesn't know the extent of influence the church's educational program has had on her. She is aware of growth in her ability to raise ethical issues at work and in school. She has discovered that she teaches ethics in her biology courses. She can't help it. Nothing in life is separated from God's purposes in creation. While she doesn't feel like an expert on God's ethical purpose, she is cognizant of her understanding of God's purpose in her life.

Her husband has been as affected by the church's educational process as she. His values and spiritual growth have developed with hers during the years they were together in the program before they were married. They continued to participate after marriage. The kinds of courses they choose now are somewhat different from their choices before they married. They are grateful that their congregation has a selection of courses from which they can choose.

A part of the education program has been the emphasis on ministry through her career. Jill has been intrigued by the possibilities her teaching and research have opened. She has taught in the adult education classes at church. She, with the encouragement of church leaders, also offered a course in genetic ethics and another on the ethical foundation for biological research in a community school for adults. She would never have considered making these latter courses available without urging from her congregation.

One of the aspects of her and her husband's decision to move into the city is her desire to work with some of the disadvantaged as well as the affluent people in her new neighborhood. She feels her training in health care, family planning, and nutrition will be useful to both groups. She intends to volunteer a few hours each week to get this program going in the congregation they have selected. They have received approval for starting the program from the governing body of the church.

Jill and her husband considered giving two years as missionaries in another part of the nation. After considering this option, they decided to work in their own way as members of a city congregation. They were supported in this decision by their peers in their church. While the church offered several other opportunities for career people to be involved in active mission, Jill and her husband chose to devote their time to a program they could initiate and manage. This decision was the basis for creating the proposal eventually accepted by the congregation to which they are moving.

They are going to miss the monthly neighborhood discussion group. It hasn't been as influential in their decision making as their fellowship group at church, but it has added a uniquely theological dimension to their lives. Neighborhoods are not ideal combinations of people, but as long as the issues dealt with were ethics and theological implications of life patterns, the interchanges added much to Jill's spiritual reservoir.

Among those who attended these discussions were several sets of new parents. She learned from them some things to expect when her child is born. She would probably have found these things out later, but it was nice to talk about them with people her age who had just gone through the birthing process.

Of the experiences in the church she has found rewarding, being a leader has been the best. She likes to teach and to organize. She is competent in leading people. This competency has been nurtured at work, but it was mellowed by her church duties. She learned patience at church. She has been taught that everyone's viewpoint must be listened to. She has accepted the fact that hasty decisions lead to disgruntled people who insist that a small group is trying to run the church.

Being a leader has been good for Jill. It helped her move from adolescent to young adult to adult. She can't put a date on when she became an adult, but being appointed to the adult education committee her second year out of college was a milestone. All at once she had to think and plan like an adult. Without such an opportunity, she would not have been forced to see herself as a productive adult person.

The church has performed its roles well during Jill's lifetime. She knows other people have fallen away and been lost to congregations because of the church's lack of concern or disciplined programming. She is thankful that that hasn't happened to her and wants to do her best to make certain it happens less frequently in the future. This twenty-eight year old has goals and values that include the church even while they center on her family. This is a strong beginning for an adult life.

SEVEN

The Long Haul
Beginning in 2010

Jill is in her early thirties in 2010. She, like at least 60 percent of the women in the nation, has an established career, a marriage, and a one-child family. She will have two more children if she is like the average, married, career woman of 2010.

She has life goals that will guide her decision making in the future. She has worked hard at creating a strong relationship with her husband and wants to keep it for the remainder of her life. Family stability has been an important social value for the past two decades. The way young couples like Jill and her husband are working at their relationships, the number of divorces will recede even further in the years ahead.

Jill has come to understand that the future is uncertain. Although she doesn't relish them, she accepts instability and insecurity as normal ingredients of life. For one thing, international terrorism has become a serious problem even in the United States. One of Jill's colleagues from the research lab was killed in a bomb explosion when she was visiting in New York. Jill didn't know what the group responsible for the bomb wanted; she knew only her anger. Her subsequent decision was not to visit New York. She is happy that her husband doesn't have to go there even on business.

She depends on her husband, her parents, and her peer group at church for most of her support. She has retained two close friends from her college days, a few friends from her former place of residence, and one close associate at her job. While she has narrowed her friendship clique by focusing it, she tries to maintain friendly contacts with a wide range of acquaintances. She has learned that being affiliated with a number of social groups is useful, but she doesn't depend on the social groups' advice or counsel for life-changing choices.

She works at teaching, having given up her research job when her child was born. Now she works full time, in spite of the couple's earlier decision for her to work part time, in a private high school in the suburbs. She quit the public system because it became so encumbered with politics that she felt it had lost sight of its ultimate purpose. She enjoys the research facilities open to her at a nearby laboratory. This business allows teachers to use equipment and resources for doing experiments so long as any discoveries they make become the company's joint property. This situation is ideal for Jill. It lets her keep involved in research while teaching full time.

Helping with the housework and attending to child care have been easy adjustments for Jill and her husband. They feel, like most of their peers, that family members must do their tasks jointly. Society has blunted the sex-stereotyped roles Jill knew in her family years ago. Men are as involved with housework and child care as are women. At least a fourth of the husbands Jill knows work part time in order to allow their wives to follow a full-time career.

Sometimes she is envious of her friends who chose not to have children. They seem to have time to do so much! However, as she counts them, she discovers they are a minority of married women. When she was in college, experts were predicting a significant increase in the number of couples who would have no children. This prediction didn't come true. Women were able to combine work and family more easily because men reshaped their roles. Childless couples are a rarity.

Jill has kept up her exercising, and her husband keeps trim. They are careful of their diet and take advantage of the nutrition sections that take up half of the food stores. These contain several types of dried and packaged foods rich in vitamins and nutrients. These sections in stores have increased in size during

the past decade, probably as a direct result of the innovations
in food preparation for space travel.

Space travel is still limited to business people because of
costs. Few ordinary folks, like Jill, can afford the luxury of
going halfway around the globe in an hour. The vehicle is like
a spaceship of a few years back and travels in a suborbit. It is
exceptionally fast. Jill and her husband have toyed with the
idea of saving money for a vacation and using the spaceship
for one leg of the journey. This, they admit, is wishful thinking.

Their conventional travel is done by personal auto. They
choose this means rather than commercial methods because
they like to go to places off the beaten path. They carefully
select vacation spots, often in nonurban sites, where they can
hike or relax at their leisure. They do not like resorts that are
popular for people their age because of the extensive leisure
activities in such places for each member of the family. Neither
have they invested in a vacation home like several of their
affluent friends. They prefer to choose without constraints where
they spend time together.

Jill, though no longer working as a biogenetic researcher, has
kept up with innovations in genetics through experimentation
and study. She fears extensive control over biogenetic research
by the chemical industry. Several large chemical firms have
recently merged with biogenetic research businesses. As a consequence, those who control chemicals and whose track record
in industrial pollution has not been exemplary, now control
genetic research. The combination of chemistry and biogenetics
can be fatal, from her perspective, to the free development of
humans. She knows from inside experience the frightful gene
mutants that can be produced in a laboratory. With few re-
straints on its research activities, the chemical and biogenetic
industry can become a menace to life as she knows it.

She utilizes the day-care nursery in the public elementary
school next to the private high school where she teaches. Jill
and her husband decided on this facility rather than any of the
commercial day-care centers in town because they wanted a
good learning environment for their child. In twenty years of
experience, the public school center has learned how best to
surround young children with a caring and instructional set-

ting. Jill appreciates this experience because she remembers her own feelings about the baby-sitting type of center she attended when she was a preschooler.

She is pleased with her decision to move closer to her parents. They have been helpful in decision making and are establishing grandparent roles for Jill's child. She recognizes the slowdown in their activity level and notices that their illnesses and sore muscles stay with them longer. Age, something she had not thought much about before, is beginning to appear in the faces and actions of her parents. They aren't feeble, but they remind her that life is not just for the young.

Her parents decided not to move to Sun Belt climes because the cities there have the problems and crime associated in earlier decades with northern cities. Instead they have chosen to move into a small town not far from their former home. The medical facilities in this community are excellent and have special care units especially for elderly patients. Jill's parents do not anticipate moving into a nursing home but will consider one of the more homelike care facilities that have been established during the past fifteen years. Jill is pleased with their planning partly because they have indicated she will not be responsible for their housing or care during their declining years.

Telecommunications is her husband's field and it continues to grow. World libraries, international shopping, and electronic meetings of world experts are commonplace. As a result, some of the emphasis on nationalism has been blunted and an interdependent world economy is closer to reality than it was a decade ago. Jill can choose television programs from many countries, and the use of such programs makes several languages almost mandatory in the schools. Her Spanish has given her a broader range of television programs to view.

The advent of the home robot several years ago didn't affect Jill until it got cheaper. Now she has one that does most of the routine cleaning. It saves her much time, and she wonders how she got along without it.

Lasers have been improved and are used not only in medicine but also in the home. Of particular importance has been their use in waste disposal. The old compactors have been replaced by devices that melt both metal and glass. It then separates the metals and glass by types into compartments. Jill, whose life pattern emphasizes conservation, uses one of these waste disposals in her home. She takes the materials to the community recycling center.

Solid waste from communities is routinely used as an energy resource. Former dumps are the sites of gas wells that are drilled into in order to collect methane to be used as fuel. All metals are melted into bars and sold to international metal mills. Paper products are burned as fuel. Plastics have been replaced by recyclable glass and paper. Rubber is recycled for road building and roofing materials.

Computers are common to most households. Some homes have three or four computers, each of which is used for a different purpose. For many people, such as Jill's husband, computers have made commuting to work a sometime thing. Computers have become a necessary technology to control the electronic houses of the past decade. The jump to technological homes was not sudden; it had been evolving for half a century.

Divorce among Jill's friends has been rare. Something happened in society during her formative years that made her age group try hard to make good choices of partners and to strive for lasting relationships. Perhaps it was the unhappy childhoods of young friends that influenced their thoughts about marriage. No matter what the trigger was, the social mood surrounding her during the past decade has not tolerated, much less encouraged, divorce.

Jill is happy with the place of the church in her life. In fact, the church's influence is at an all-time high. She doesn't quite understand the reasons for the popularity of the church, but she knows how much it has meant to her over the years. At last others are finding its message useful in their lives. Not only can she go to church for the worship experience, but because worship services are broadcast over local cable stations, she can tape them for more careful listening later. This practice has increased the power of the message for her and her husband.

Jill's previous choices, carefully made and tested with trustworthy peer groups and parents, were based on life goals inclusive enough to give her growing room. As a result, she is in a much better situation than some of her friends whose goals were neither future oriented nor broad enough to allow for personal development. As she contemplates the life ahead, she knows her foundation is secure and the start she has made can be satisfying over the long haul. She will need a strong base to confront challenges in the next few years.

Revising Goals

Goals must be adjusted as a person enters each new stage of life. Jill has discovered that she must keep herself alert to the next set of demands. A second child, a change of occupation or of the amount of time worked by either Jill or her husband, moving to another home, a personal or family illness, a natural or human catastrophe, or the loss of one or more parents or other family member will demand immediate revisions of expectations and goals. She has no control over many of these events; yet they will change her life, and a significant adjustment in life will necessitate her revision of goals. Jill knows goal making is not an exercise in dreaming. Revising goals is the only way she keeps pointed in her chosen direction.

When she was in school, her goals were governed by the school calendar: she figured in four-year cycles. When she started work, she thought in the same cycle but discovered that her goal making began to coincide with changes in her life situation. Marriage, moving, and having a child were events that caused her to revise goals. She wants to continue to update her goals but knows the time schedule for revision is not always for her to determine.

She is beginning to acknowledge the strength of outside forces over which she has no control. For instance, she didn't think about the effects that marriage would have on expanding her family base. No longer can she think only about her parents, but she must consider the repercussions of her decisions on her in-laws. In addition, what happens to people at work, friends at church, and neighbors have their impact on her and her family.

Some outside events are more telling than others. For example, when her close friend was killed in an automobile accident, Jill had much difficulty explaining to herself the reason for such a mishap. She was able to verbalize a good answer to others but the internal impression it left on her was vivid.

She has recently felt vulnerable to the external forces that govern her, her child's, and her husband's lives. She felt helpless when school officials made a decision about her child's grade placement. Their choice affected her hopes and ambitions for her child. She has to adjust those aspirations even though she wished she were correct and school officials were wrong. The concept of fate began to have personal meaning for her.

She had difficulty in accepting decisions others made regarding her husband's future with his consulting network. She so identified with him that the snub he received from his colleagues insulted her as well. She knew she shouldn't feel like that, but her reactions were due partly to the resistance she has toward forces over which she has no control or influence.

Jill, because of these and similar experiences, has discovered that revisions in goals are made subtly. A few changes are instituted by other people because they have power to cut off options or choices. Most adjustments, however, she can make on her own volition.

She remains in control of her ultimate direction no matter what obstacles or detours others may place in her immediate path. She has learned that she has at least two alternatives when faced with situations demanding change: she can accept fate as a part of life and give up on planning; or she can accept fate as something over which she has no say and plan her direction on the basis of what she can control. Because she has reached this level of personal goal setting, she has matured enough to make the long haul both interesting and fulfilling.

Career Change Options

Jill's education and experience are a base from which she can move into other careers. She chose to limit her career to teaching when she had a child. She had thought she would work part time. Instead she teaches full time and takes advantage of an industry offer to allow her to continue research and experimentation in their laboratory. When a second child comes, she may opt for part-time teaching, but this seems unlikely. She has used the child-care center in the community and likes it.

It is staffed by women and men whose career is tending and training prekindergarten children. She will transfer the child at age three into the public school prekindergarten program. Then the child will be sent to private school because it has better teachers and more diverse course offerings and encourages children to progress at their own rate. Her first child is now, at age five, reading at level three. This wouldn't be possible in the public system.

Options, if she wants to change her career, will come partly from exterior forces such as the economy, the availability of people with her qualifications for selected jobs, and her husband's work situation. Other opportunities for change will spring from her personal interests, how well she does her job, and the decisions she and her husband make about having more children. Any options will arise in unexpected sequences. Jill's background will help to open opportunities if she needs to shift into another occupation or reduce her work schedule.

An unexpected option came last year when she was asked to be chairperson of the high school science department. The chairperson was retiring. She was recommended on the basis of her competence in the field, her innovative educational techniques, and her leadership qualities. In this case, a career opportunity opened because of an external event, a retirement, but the suggestion that she be appointed was a result of her experience in teaching and genetic research.

She accepted the position; however, she asked for and was granted a sabbatical. The study leave was to allow her time to take courses in educational administration. Being chairperson of the department means that she will spend more time in curricula planning and administration than in teaching. She felt that she needed additional training to make this switch more easily.

The pattern of taking time off for training in a new specialty is common in many professions. Even medical practitioners, most of whom are related to medical corporations, are granted leave time to improve their skills. In fact, the government demands that skill tests for medical specialists be taken every five years.

An indirect result of taking the position of chair of the science department is her qualification, due to courses taken during the leave, to become a principal or superintendent in the school system. The chairperson job was offered as a result of a retirement, an event external to her control. She accepted the position because she was interested in developing a revised curriculum for the high school science department. She chose to take additional courses to prepare herself for new tasks and now finds herself qualified in a different educational career track. This sequence of events was not planned. Another external event could open a job for her as an educational administrator. The interplay of external event and pursuit of internal interests are the context of career change for Jill and her colleagues.

A different set of circumstances could result in Jill's decision to quit teaching altogether. She may choose to have one or more additional children. If she is like many other career women her age, she will decide to stay home with the children during their preschool years. She might, as many others have, ask for a part-time job where she used to work.

Women, especially career persons, seek part-time jobs to keep in touch with their field. They want to return to their careers and don't want to be penalized for their choice to stay home with children for a while. Businesses encourage this practice. They have discovered the cost of losing trained and experienced people is greater than the inconvenience of part-time workers.

An important factor in Jill's career options is her husband's job. So far, she has not had to contend with a major shift in his occupation, but it is conceivable that he will want to relate more closely with a corporation rather than continue with the consulting network in the near future. The network phenomenon, popular through the late 1990s and early years of this century, is giving way to small corporations run somewhat like partnerships. The participants have more legal protections and can plan budgets and compensation more easily than they can as network members. In fact, her husband has been hinting about becoming part of such a corporation for the past year.

One implication of a change for him would include moving. If a move should occur, Jill must decide whether to move with him or to sustain a commuting family similar to those of several of her friends. Many of them are separated from their families for three or four days a week because the spouses must live in different cities. Taking care of the children in these marriages has inevitably become the responsibility of the person who has remained in the original home place. More than half of the time this has been the woman. Jill feels strongly that their child should continue to have both parents in the home most of the time.

Therefore, Jill has pushed from her mind any thought of the strains of living apart and having to make daily choices for herself and her family. She isn't willing to consider this option. She would be more willing to drop out of the job market for a time to keep the family together. She is convinced that she can find a job in one of her fields no matter where they might locate. This determination has kept the potential panic of having to start again at a minimum.

She doesn't think she can handle separation easily. Unfortunately, she will have to prepare herself for the inevitable.

Dealing With Separation and Loss

Jill hasn't faced loss through death of any of her family. Two of her grandparents are living near her parents and the other two live within a hundred miles. Her husband, on the other hand, lost one set of grandparents in an airplane accident when he was in his teens. He has some understanding of grief and anger that come as a result of the death of a loved one.

Jill's perception of her parents is beginning to change. She has had no trouble in thinking of her grandparents as old, but somehow she can't adjust her image of her parents to accept their aging. When she does, she must confront the fact that she is getting older as well. While aging is a positive attribute, she isn't certain she likes the wrinkles and increasing feebleness accompanying her parents' aging. She isn't worried about them contracting any cancer because most types are curable. However, she is very concerned about the inactivity that appears to plague older persons. She doesn't want that to happen to her folks.

The death of her friend pointed out to Jill how small her sphere of influence is. She never considered death a threat to any of her circle until the accident claimed her friend's life.

Jill's feeling of mortality increased manyfold then. She had to acknowledge the limits of being careful, purchasing a safe automobile, and obeying traffic laws. None of these had saved her friend. Even though the police said it was a freak accident, she was gone. There was no doubt in Jill's mind of the loss when she stood in the cemetary to witness the burial. The woman was gone. The friendship was ended.

Jill didn't handle the loss well. Her circumscribed world had been invaded by a force that took away a friend. Suddenly her well-planned universe was vulnerable. Of course she knew this all along, but suffering a loss made her very aware of her limits. Her goals had been well thought out, and her energies had been focused. But so had those of her friend, and now she was gone. Was the God who listened to her not one of love and care? If so, what had happened to God's care of her friend?

It had been a difficult three months following the funeral. The loss was devastating not only because of the loss of her friend but because of the questions the loss raised. One of these days she was going to lose other friends or even face death herself. These were not comforting thoughts.

At thirty-three, Jill is older than most people who have to deal with separation and loss. Divorce has created hardships on a few of her friends. She has watched them try to revitalize their lives. It was hard even though most of them had sympathetic and supportive friends. Separation is one of the most difficult events for people to handle, at least from Jill's viewpoint. Her response, finally, was to turn to her support groups— her husband, parents, and church—for the strength she needed. Each gave her insight into living through the initial pangs of being separated from loved ones and the eventual loss of those a person loves the most.

On the other hand, Jill has a strong foundation that will allow her to accept even the most difficult situation and turn it into a positive experience. The lesson in handling grief by turning to her family and friends will stand her in good stead. Her willingness to discuss how she felt about the loss of a friend convinced her that she was not alone in either her questioning nor her faith. The bleakness of burial provided reality to the finality of death. She found the total experience comforting even though its harshness was not covered up. Acceptance of death was possible, and at her age she had to know that.

Revising Their Life-Style

Jill and her husband like to live simply. They are a conserving couple. They dislike pretentiousness and display. However, they moved to the suburbs and have had to change their ways somewhat. They chose the suburb because it was supportive of their life pattern. It was well served by public transit; it was limited in size; it had a community focus in a park and recreational area; and it boasted a good complex of schools including university extension campuses.

The auto that served them in the city remains their only car. Jill uses it to get to work and to take their child to the preschool learning center. Her husband uses public transit to commute to work twice a week. Their ideas about conservation and energy have been bolstered by the attitude in this community toward recycling.

The change in jobs by her husband jolted their life-style considerably. They had to adjust to his commute even though it is only twice a week. Jill, because of the current teacher shortage, found a position in the private high school. They enrolled their child in the nearby preschool center. They must go into the nearby city regularly for social functions sponsored by her husband's company, and this requirement presses into their schedule. They are reluctant for him to go alone since these social events, reversing a trend of the 1990s, are designed to include spouses.

A complication of his new job is the increased clothing expense for both of them. They were able to get by with casual dress so long as he worked at home more than half the time and she taught in a modest city neighborhood school. They had few social obligations then. Now they must dress well when they attend social functions because it is expected. They hadn't counted on this and discover themselves resisting the implied requirement. They found, on their first encounter at such a function, that the social demands of the occasion does not allow for personal deviations. Thus they had to purchase clothes appropriate to attend these functions. Even so, they were the most conservatively dressed couple present.

Shopping is different in the suburbs. When they go to the local stores, to shop, people know them. They are not protected by the anonymity of the masses as they were in the city. Additionally, the choice of places to shop is limited even though the merchandise is high quality. The availability of clothing more in keeping with their life-style has to be ordered by computer or purchased in one of the malls a few miles away. They don't mind the drive to the malls, but the traffic makes the time spent on the road to get there and back a concern.

They have been invited into neighbors' homes, which is another difference between the city and this suburb. They had thought the individuality that people prized would be more evident in a suburb than in a city, but they were disappointed. They enjoyed the standoffishness of city people and are uncomfortable with the expectation that they are to host get-togethers for neighbors. This is part of the suburban life-style they don't enjoy much, and they are prefunctorily fulfilling their obligations. As soon as the first round of parties is finished, they intend to be quite selective in who they entertain.

They have found a church that meets most of their criteria. Its adult education program isn't as good as the one in their last church, but it offers a choice between three classes. The focus is on Bible study, but the teachers relate current issues to biblical themes. The class they chose has a range of age groups in it and seems to be the type of mix from which they can get much. Two neighborhood families belong to the church, and one couple is in the class. A strong friendship might work out with them.

Peer pressure is very strong in the community. Unspoken rules of etiquette and protocol are communicated quietly in half sentences during casual conversations. Neighbors and people from the church suggest appropriate shopping places, barber shops, doctors, restaurants, and types of entertainment. Jill and her husband are independent and like to think they are capable of making these decisions without external assistance. On the other hand, they must live in this community with these people as neighbors and friends. Therefore, they take the suggestions.

Jill is finding, in these experiences, the meaning of forced change. Her and her husband's decision was to move to a place and to continue to live as they had in the past. This isn't possible. People are social entities and develop group life patterns. While these life-styles are not adhered to completely by everyone, the general pattern is evident. Groups, therefore, have a life pattern which is imposed on newcomers. Subtle pressures, such as exclamations in conversations, critical comments, and not inviting the deviants to neighborhood and church gatherings, alert new residents to acceptable behavior. Jill has had to adjust her thinking about living her own life in order to become flexible enough to fit in with the new groups.

Building on a Solid Foundation

Nothing from her past experience can be used as a foolproof guide to decision making in her present. She could rely on herself when she was single, but decisions then were uncomplicated by a family. She had only herself to worry about. Now every choice she makes, including purchasing a coat, must be weighed by the consequences it has on her child and her husband. She doesn't feel weighted down by this, but the process for selecting what she and they do is much more different than any she utilized in the past.

As a result, she has drastically altered her decision-making procedure. Now, before they are finalized, her choices in most things are discussed with her husband as his are with her. They have discovered that even the smallest decision can create friction between them. This is especially true on days when events at work have been trying or when they don't feel well. This doesn't mean that they can't make decisions. Each knows the other person can see consequences each may have overlooked.

They are intent upon pursuing their personal careers and goals. They aren't afraid to be individuals and can handle the ensuing conflict in family conversations. As they work through their individual desires and hopes, they are forging a new basis for their lives. The separate life goals and expectations they had before marriage are slowly being revised to include each other. As a result, they are beginning to form another set of goals that incorporate their individual ones and express hopes for their life together. They are surprised that this procedure of building family goals has taken so long. What they will discover is that the process continues as long as they remain a family.

The first years together were exploratory for Jill and her husband. They learned to appreciate each other, to understand some of the internal expectations and ambitions of the partner, to applaud the strengths and to recognize the weaknesses of the other, and they created a forum in which they can share. Jill and her husband might not analyze their beginning family years in these words. They might insist they had been laying a solid foundation for the years ahead. Both descriptions of their experiences lead to the same conclusion—without an understanding of each other and a joint desire to share life's decisions, their marriage will not last. They must have a strong basis on which to build later experiences because stress and strain will be present throughout life.

Two facts stand out in Jill's mind. First, she and her husband must share everything in life if they are going to maintain a viable family. Second, their individual desires must be tailored to the realities of living with appreciation and consideration for each other. These facts have been taught to them by peers, friends who have gone through divorces, and the church. The family council around the dinner table began early in the marriage. Jill insists on it as a time when difficult choices as well as triumphs and disappointments are shared. Dinner time gives them a chance to think through each other's reactions and suggestions before going to bed. Anger and conflict are much easier for them to handle after a cooling-off period and before retiring.

Neither feels free to decide arbitrarily on a career option without consulting with and considering its implications on the other. Both are working people with long-term career goals. They want to be successful and respected among colleagues in their field. They want to see results from their work. These are strong forces pushing both of them. Yet they covenanted when they married that both should pursue their chosen livelihoods as long as they desired. They respect and uphold that covenant.

These agreements and feelings toward each other are elements in the foundation of their marriage. The two people may not consciously acknowledge the importance of their feelings about the covenant or their attitude about sharing decisions, but they do know when either violates an agreement or ignores the time of sharing. A solid foundation for marriage is built in degrees, and each year either adds to or detracts from its strength. Jill and her husband's commitment to keep the basis for their lives strong is an essential part of the roots for their marriage. No one outside themselves will eventually be responsible for the kind of family life they have nor of the kind of children they raise. The results of their commitment to each other and the solidity of their marriage's foundation will be the major factors in both.

Testing Reality

Jill's teaching environment in the suburb is quite different from the city school system she left. The diversity of people and values she confronted in the city is not evident in this suburb. People of various races and cultures are present, but they seem to function on the same value system. She isn't certain that the community values are appropriate for herself or her family. Yet she has begun to feel a certain security in her life here. She wonders about herself and her own values.

The edge of tension she feels is healthy. Jill's values must be her own if she intends to follow the purpose and goals that she and her husband have set for their family. She will realize shortly that her values will be in tension with those held by most others with whom she works and associates. If she continues to live in a suburb, the values held by the residents will clash often with her conservative and spartan ideas about life. She will resist the display and abhor some of the opulent tenor of affluence of some residents. At the same time, she will enjoy the suburb's benefits, including its schools, parks, recreation areas, and wages.

Being part of a social situation doesn't mean that a person accepts everything about it. Jill can continue to teach her values informally in class the same as other teachers share theirs. She can resist personal display and insensitive use of money by channeling her family's resources into church activities and missions. She can criticize existing values by her life-style and approach to living. She can speak out when she sees others being injured by inappropriate pressures or actions. She can do any of these things as a protest to accepted values, but she must decide to act and then do the actions on her own. No one is going to invite or make her resist them.

Taking the initiative to test her ideas of reality is not new to Jill. She is certain of her concept of reality. She knows the way people live and think in this suburb is not representative of many others. She is in an enclave. Somehow she must keep in touch with other situations in order to find a corrective to the environment in which she lives. She does this by traveling, visiting, and studying. Her aim is to fight any unconscious acceptance of the life-style of those around her.

She finds support for her resistance in her husband and among a few persons at church. She is dismayed that many church people accept the life patterns dominant in the community without question. She finds it difficult to remember that their capitulation to an easy life doesn't mean that she must accept it. Therefore, she pushes for changes in church programs to include exchanges with other churches, support for missions dealing with other cultures, and adult education courses explaining Christian life patterns.

As she becomes involved in these church activities, she discovers again the importance of peers who think like her. She is frustrated easily, but with others encouraging her, she can do much more than she thought. With her husband joining her, she finds new meaning to the phrase "joint action." Others might be able to work against large odds by themselves but Jill cannot. She must have support.

The church has once again become a critical part of Jill's life. She must have its help as she lives in any setting. The people in the church are not saints nor do all of them believe as she does, but the basic values and attitudes among these people support hers.

The Church's Role

Several of Jill's friends are beginning to return to the church after dropping out during their twenties. She feels fortunate because her church has made a point of keeping in touch with her and has made certain that she remained active in a congregation. In fact, she has been a member of three different congregations since she left home to attend college. The home congregation, however, has been the continuing contact and guide over the years.

The roles of the church now include educator for her child, educator of herself and her husband, a source of strength for her values, a provider of fellowship. In addition, the church provides opportunities for her to be a leader. The congregation lets her know that she and her family are valued members. Jill feels surrounded by love and care in spite of the normal frictions and disagreements that are part of church life.

Perhaps the most important group at present is the fellowship one. Most of the members are her age and deal with similar problems at work and at home. She and her husband can, in congenial conversation with them, explore ways to approach difficult decisions, learn how to handle awkward work and neighborhood situations, understand some of the expectations of the residents toward newcomers, and get helpful hints for child raising. They are not close friends with any particular couple, but the general atmosphere makes sharing easy and informative.

The adult education program serves quite a different function for them than does the fellowship group. The intent of adult education, from Jill's perspective, is to inform and provide a discussion forum. Resource leaders from the congregation as well as experts in various fields, regardless of church affiliation, are utilized as teachers. The courses are designed by each class, which makes the selection of the class to attend very important. She and her husband have chosen carefully and are active in helping to design as well as lead their class.

Testing and strengthening values occur during class, at fellowship meetings, and at worship. She finds the opportunity to receive and exchange ideas to be a necessary corollary to her teaching. When she teaches, no one challenges her values. At church people do challenge her values, and she knows this is important even though it is painful at times. Without this testing of attitudes, values, and life pattern, she can be lulled into

believing that everything she does is God's will. She is quite
aware of her fallibility.

Jill sees opportunities for leadership in the church as ways
to learn and to grow. She doesn't view leadership as an obligation or a necessity. She carefully picks where she will spend
her time because she wants to make it count. Even though she
turns down more positions than she accepts, she doesn't feel
at all guilty. She believes that the church needs many different
people as leaders if it is to accomplish its tasks.

As she looks into the future, Jill is certain that she and her
husband can withstand and overcome whatever it holds. She
is not cavalier about their strength but bases her feelings upon
what they have done and how they have worked out their
decisions. She knows where to turn for help and relies on
certain groups for support. Her faith has been started well, and
she feels comfortable with her values. She is willing to live
with their decisions and is confident that God will lead them
in the days coming. Her steadfastness is not without misgivings.
These she shares with her husband. They covenant again to
work together to live a useful life as partners.

Epilogue

We first met Jill as an eight year old and leave her as a thirty-
three-year-old working mother. We have been with her at key
decision points and have watched some of the consequences
of those choices. She has been fortunate during these years
because the church has kept in touch with her. Some of her
friends have had a much more difficult time in keeping their
lives on track because their church set them adrift early in their
teen years.

Jill will face many of the same emotions and feelings in later
years that she has confronted during the time we've been with
her. In the years ahead, however, she will have her own example
to refer to as a base for new choices and actions. Her foundation
has been established, and she is as ready as most of us for the
long haul, the life yet to be lived.

Resources

Magazines

"What the Next 50 Years Will Bring," *U.S. News & World Report*, May 9, 1983.

Books

Baier, Kurt, and Rescher, Nicholas, eds., *Values and the Future.* New York: The Free Press, 1969.

Harman, Willis W., *An Incomplete Guide to the Future.* San Francisco: San Francisco Book Co., Inc., 1976.

Johnson, Carroll, and Johnson, Douglas W., *Religion in America: 1950 to the Present.* New York: Harper and Row Publishers, Inc., 1979.

Kahn, Herman, et al., *The Next Two Hundred Years.* New York: William Morrow & Co., Inc., 1976.

Moffitt, Donald, ed., *The Wall Street Journal Views America Tomorrow.* Princeton, New Jersey: Dow Jones Books, 1977.

Naisbitt, John, *Megatrends: Ten New Directions Transforming Our Lives.* New York: Warner Books, Inc., 1982.

Toffler, Alvin, *The Third Wave.* New York: William Morrow and Co., Inc., 1980.

Other

The United States Census report is a continuing source of information and projection. Anyone looking at the future must keep track of the data in this report.

Two magazines regularly contain useful information about trends and issues shaping the future: *U.S. News and World Report* and *The Futurist*.

The magazine, *Psychology Today*, publishes useful articles on human behavior and adaptation. These articles can be used to project future events and behavior changes.

Specific projections in the book have been based primarily on data from Project Outlook Events—1982. This is the report of a continuing Delphi project sponsored by the Center for Futures Research of the Graduate School of Business, University of Southern California. The projections I used are derived from summary data of Questionnaire I, Spring, 1983.

Two newspapers regularly include data and projections useful for developing scenarios of the future: *The Wall Street Journal* and *U.S.A. Today*.